© 2024 by Stas Jamie

All rights reserved. No part of this book may be reproduced, stored in a retrieval system, or transmitted in any form or by any means, electronic, mechanical, photocopying, recording, or otherwise, without the prior written permission of the publisher, except in the case of brief quotations embodied in critical articles and reviews.

Published by Amazon

First Edition

Cover design by Stas Jamie

- Introduction 8
- What the hell is a Sasquatch? 10
- Men or Ape 17
- Native Tales of the "Hairy Man" 19
  - Shocking Tales: Early Sightings by Settlers 22
- Where can I find Bigfoot 26
  - Bigfoot Hotspots of the Pacific Northwest 26
  - Revisiting the Patterson Film Site 29
  - Preserving the Sanctuary 30
  - The Volcano Habitat of Mount St. Helens 34
  - Epicenter of the Unknown: The Skookum Meadows Habitat 37
  - Bigfoot Hotspot: Salt Fork State Park 40
  - The Swamp Ape: Florida's Bigfoot 42
  - British Columbia's Habitats 44
  - When Giants Attack: The Harrison Hot Springs Habitat 47
  - The Harrison Lake Region 47
  - Epicenter of Encounters: The Fraser Canyon Habitat 49
- Sasquatch Capital of Eastern Canada: Northern Ontario's Overlooked Habitats 53
- Alaska's Overlooked Wildmen: The Panhandle's Prime Habitat 56
  - The Panhandle Coast 56
  - Alaska's Forgotten Wildmen: The Interior's Prime Habitat 58
- What Sasquatch Eats 60

- Migration Theories 62
- Bigfoot worldwide 64
  - Yeti 64
  - China's Elusive Wildman 67
  - The Yowie 70
  - The Almas 72
- Supernatural Tales: Bigfoot's Paranormal Powers 74
  - Vanishing into Thin Air 76
  - A Sixth Sense for Danger 77
  - Interdimensional Travelers 77
  - Conversations With No Words 79
  - Mysteries in the Forest 84
  - Phantoms From Another Realm 87
- The sightings 90
  - Breaking Down the Patterson Footage 90
  - Patterson's Other Encounters 92
  - Examining the Memorial Day Footage 94
  - Scrutinizing the Jacobs Photos 95
  - Breaking Down the Skookum Cast 98
  - London Tracks Riddle 99
  - Sierra Sounds: Bigfoot Language? 101
  - The Frightening Bauman Incident 103

- Breaking Down William Roe's Sighting ... 104
- Albert Ostman's Abduction Story ... 105
- Teddy Roosevelt's Bigfoot Tale ... 107
- The Chilling Ruby Creek Incident ... 108
- The Mysterious Bossburg Tracks ... 110
- The Night Siege of Ape Canyon ... 111
- The Prince of Wales Bigfoot Incident ... 112
- The Botched Estes Park Capture ... 114

The evidence ... 116
- Bigfoot's Footsteps: Analyzing Sasquatch Tracks ... 116
- Dr. Jeff Meldrum's Bigfoot Print Analysis ... 120
- Rover Grantz ... 123
- Fur and Hair ... 127
- The Ketchum DNA Study: A Watershed Moment for Bigfoot Research ... 129
- The BFRO Hair Samples: Tantalizing Clues and Cautionary Tales ... 133
- Hair Samples from the Enigmatic Skookum Cast ... 137
- Bigfoot vocalizations and sound recordings ... 142

Bigfoot Nests and Shelters ... 155
- Tracking Bigfoot Home: The Olympic Project Nest Discovery ... 159

Deciphering Bigfoot's Tree Knocking Code ... 164

The Controversial Science of Sasquatch Scat ... 168

Reading the Signs of Sasquatch in the Wilderness ... 171

Reading the Outlines Left Behind in Remote Wilderness 175
The Tantalizing Quest for Sasquatch Genetic Proof 179
Bigfoot research teams 182
    Inside BFRO: The World's Leading Bigfoot Hunting Organization 182
    The North American Wood Ape Conservancy 184
    The Sasquatch Genome Project Controversy 187
    The Olympic Project: Seeking Proof in Washington's Remote Peninsula 189
Why No Body? 192
    The Everlasting Mystery of Missing Sasquatch Remains 192
Conclusion 196
    Connecting the Strands of a Compelling Mystery 196

Introduction

I want to extend my deepest gratitude to you, the reader, for purchasing this book on the mysteries surrounding the legendary creature known as Bigfoot or Sasquatch. By deciding to read this book with an open mind, you're embarking on a fascinating journey to examine compelling evidence that suggests these beings exist, defying many scientific conventions in the process.

My aim in writing this book is to present you with insightful stories, perplexing footprints, intriguing behaviors, and ground-breaking DNA analysis related to Bigfoot. All of this evidence stacks up to build a convincing case that there is an undiscovered species of primate lurking in the remote forests of North America. After reading this book cover to cover, my hope is that you walk away thoroughly convinced that the Bigfoot phenomena deserves more meaningful scientific inquiry.

While many dismiss Bigfoot as a silly myth or hoax, native tribes have told intriguing tales about hairy wild men in the woods for centuries. Even the earliest European explorers to the New World heard shocking accounts from indigenous people about giant man-like beasts that left massive footprints and terrified witnesses with bone-chilling howls. These stories were passed down through generations well before the famous Patterson-Gimlin film in 1967 that showed a lumbering, ape-like creature strolling along a creek bed.

The Patterson film brought Bigfoot into the public consciousness, sparking feverish debate between skeptics who dismiss the film as a man in an ape suit versus believers who insist the creature shows anatomical details no human could replicate. And the sightings continue today, with the Bigfoot Field Researchers Organization logging thousands of reports, with hotspots in Pacific Northwest forests.

So if these creatures are lurking in our forests, why has no body ever been found? Why do we only have photos and videos that seem inconclusive? The fact is the wilderness where Bigfoot dwells is dense and treacherous, spanning thousands of square miles. The breeding population is likely very small, making bodies exceedingly rare to find before decomposition sets in. Many sightings occur unexpectedly, leaving witnesses scrambling for cameras. And hoaxes do occur, complicating legitimate evidence.

But while the gold standard of a body continues to elude us, that does not mean compelling evidence does not exist. In this book, we will methodically walk through the voluminous sighting reports, analyze famous footage, and scrutinize biological samples through the lens of science. I will present interviews with credible witnesses and opinions from experts in primatology and anthropology. And we will explore theories related to evolution and native legends that could explain how such a creature has evaded detection for so long.

My goal by the final chapter is to provide you with sufficient evidence to walk away convinced, beyond a reasonable doubt, that a relic population of Gigantopithecus, an ancient 10 foot tall primate, never went extinct in North America but adapted superb camouflage and elusive habits to avoid humans. I aim to demonstrate through science and reason that Bigfoot is likely an undiscovered primate species, not a paranormal entity or collective delusion.

I ask that you read this book with an open and discerning mind, setting aside knee-jerk judgements as we scrutinize evidence objectively. You may not agree with every conclusion I present. But my hope is that the aggregated evidence paints a compelling picture that leaves you convinced the Bigfoot phenomena warrants deeper scientific investigation using the latest technologies and techniques. There is still much to learn about these elusive creatures, but this book will go a long way toward pulling back the veil of mystery surrounding Sasquatch.

The pages ahead promise to reshape your assumptions through persuasive stories and facts. I thank you again for joining me on this journey toward rational discovery of an allegedly mythical beast that science has refused to seriously study for decades. I hope you enjoy it as much as I enjoyed researching and writing it! Now let's begin peeling back the layers of this fascinating cryptid.

What the hell is a Sasquatch?

The contemporary notion of Bigfoot in popular culture paints a picture of a lumbering, primitive beast lurking in the ancient forests of the Pacific Northwest. But in Native American oral traditions, the wildman goes by names like Sasquatch, Skookum, or Seatco and is depicted in a more reverential light. He is not merely a relic ape, but an intelligent keeper of the land acting as a guide between the material and spiritual worlds.

According to the indigenous tribes of North America, Sasquatch stands between 8 to 15 feet tall, covered in hair, with broad shoulders and the strength to uproot trees. In that sense, the contemporary Bigfoot hunter and ancient Native shaman would recognize the same tremendous, intimidating creature. But the Native traditions suggest that the Sasquatch possesses advanced intelligence, psychic intuition, and the ability to communicate telepathically or through eerie screams. They are not mere apes, but an entity that heralds messages from other dimensions.

For example, the Lummi tribe near the Canadian border honors Ts'emekwes, the Sasquatch who acts as a teacher of ancient wisdom. Local medicine men described initiations where the hairy wildman materialized to share shamanic secrets regarding power animals before vanishing without a trace. Across the Cascades, the Sts'Ailes people tell of a tall Burnt Bridge Creek demon called sásq'ets that shouted ominous warnings about impending disasters or the deaths of tribal members.

And the famous Chief Sealth, for whom Seattle is named, recounted a boyhood vision quest where he met protective mountain spirits known as skookums that taught him sacred songs still used in tribal rituals before he became a powerful shaman. For Chief Sealth's people, the skookum was no ordinary beast, but a respected messenger between cosmic planes that appears in times of need.

For countless generations, Native tribes have viewed Sasquatch as a supernatural protector of the land, not unlike the Abominable Snowman of the Himalayas called yeti.

The highly respected medicine man John Lame Deer claimed his people consulted with the Sasquatch on major decisions and considered them sacred elders just below the Creator in status. He even insisted Native Americans originated from an ancestral tribe of Sasquatch tens of thousands of years ago.

While the Native legends seem fantastical through modern eyes, they speak to an underlying respect, even reverence, for these wildmen in the woods. The tribes viewed the Sasquatch as intelligent, cunning, and powerful beings to appease, not mindless animals to hunt or destroy. They were the sentient guardians of the magical land, using psychic abilities to avoid contact except with the most virtuous tribal members. Like any great mystery, the Sasquatch entered tribal culture as objects of wonder, not derision.

The Native legends also suggest why Sasquatch sightings seem so supernatural and reality-defying today. The wildmen utilize psychic powers, telepathy, and interdimensional travel to avoid leaving hard evidence of their existence. They make appearances during pivotal moments as shamanic spirit guides then retreat back into the shadows. They have no interest in modern technology or buildings, preferring to live as one with nature. This paints a far richer portrait of Sasquatch than the dull caricature of an aimless ape bumbling through the woods.

Of course, the traditional indigenous view of Sasquatch is deeply mystical, transmitted across generations in sacred storytelling around flickering campfires. Tales grow taller with each telling, facts mix with fantasy until they become inseparable. But the core descriptions of Sasquatch remain remarkably consistent between tribes scattered across thousands of miles: a giant hairy wildman at home in the woods, possessing human-like intelligence and otherworldly talents.

Perhaps in this modern scientific age, we have lost the capacity to believe in anything beyond what our five basic senses detect. We have traded wonder for skepticism and cold hard facts. The magical thinking of ancient tribes seems obsolete now. But a growing body of sightings, footprints, and DNA evidence suggests there could be an actual, physical creature behind the Native legends...one that science has simply failed to catalog in its arrogance.

So while the Native views of Sasquatch seem mystical compared to our clinical notions of reality, the truth may reside somewhere in between the magic and mundane. We must broaden our narrow definitions of what constitutes life on this strange planet to make room for the possibility that we have missed entire species hidden in plain sight. And science must humbly return to those who lived closest to the land since time immemorial for clues.

The Native elders speak with conviction rooted in oral histories millennia old. Their Sasquatch is no mere animal, but an intelligent entity straddling multiple planes of existence. This does not fit neatly into the modern zoological taxonomy, yet the stories persist through centuries of colonization and cultural genocide. As we examine the evidence in later chapters, let us keep an open mind to indigenous beliefs in case they reveal truths modern society has forgotten in our haste to conquer nature. For if Sasquatch does exist, science has much to learn from cultures that never severed their primal connection to the wilderness.

While no Bigfoot has been conclusively studied in captivity, sighting reports over the past century suggest these mysterious creatures exhibit a number of consistent behaviors and share certain physical traits. By aggregating the observations of alleged witnesses, researchers have pieced together profiles of these elusive creatures even if science refuses to acknowledge their existence.

In terms of behavior, Bigfoot creatures seem to be largely nocturnal, preferring to forage and travel at night while bedding down in crude forest nests during the day. They are always sighted in remote wilderness areas, suggesting an aversion to humans and human activity. They appear to be omnivorous, feeding on berries, nuts, and small animals. Bigfoot travel in small family groups of around 5-10 members and may communicate using wood knocks, rock clacks, and piercing howls. Witnesses describe stealthy movement through thick forests, suggesting familiarity with their dense habitat.

Regarding physical form, the majority of sightings describe Bigfoot as bipedal creatures covered in hair that stand between 6-10 feet tall and weigh 400-800 pounds. They have broad shoulders, no neck, and a conical head that sits directly atop the trapezius muscles. Long arms nearly reach the knees and powerful legs drive locomotion. The face lacks prominent brow ridges but has a flat, wide nose and dark, deeply set eyes beneath a heavy brow.

Some witnesses report a strong, unpleasant odor accompanying Bigfoot, akin to rotten eggs or the musk of an animal. This makes sense given the thick hair covering that likely harbors bacteria in the absence of regular grooming practices. The hair coat itself ranges from black, brown, auburn, grey, and white-silver. The variation suggests regional adaptations akin to human ethnicities. And debunkers take note - no Bigfoot has ever been reported with neatly trimmed or styled face and head hair as one would expect in a prankster in a costume.

In terms of lifestyle, Bigfoot lead a primitive existence as forest dwellers, lacking any clothing, tools, or shelter beyond crude stick nests. They change locations often, never staying more than a few days in one area. Their nomadic lifestyle keeps them on the move foraging for sustenance over a large territory spanning hundreds of square miles.

Bigfoot creatures display advanced intelligence and self-preservation instincts. They are almost always spotted first by witnesses and vanish quickly before any clear photograph can emerge. They avoid roads, structures, and humans at all costs, wanting no interaction with civilization. These behaviors suggest cunning animals with reasoning skills aware of the dangers that humans pose.

Perhaps the most intriguing trait of Bigfoot is their eerie screams. Witnesses consistently describe terrifying shrieks, wails, and cries echoing through the night, instilling primal fear. Some linguists who have analyzed the bizarre recordings estimate the vocal range spans eight octaves - three times that of humans. The unique non-human vocalizations defy easy categorization, but carry an urgent, unnerving tonality.

So while no specimen has been confirmed, a fairly consistent profile emerges from thousands of alleged sightings that flesh out subtle details regarding how Bigfoot look, act, sound and live. Of course, skeptics dismiss this as imagination run wild or people misidentifying bears. But the remarkable consistency across reports compiled worldwide suggests otherwise. It paints a portrait of an undiscovered species that displays intelligence, family bonds, communication, and survival skills specially adapted to forest life.

And the Native legends lend credence to the alleged behaviors as well. Indigenous tribes speak of powerful, wild hairy creatures dwelling deep in mountain forests, possessing uncanny abilities to avoid human detection. Intriguingly, no tribe depicts tales of capturing or killing a Sasquatch, only fleeting sightings that shocked and terrified witnesses. Much like modern sighting accounts, Native stories indicate the creatures demonstrate almost supernatural talents hidden in the shadows.

Ultimately, the lack of hard evidence leaves the accuracy of these reported behaviors and traits unproven. We are left to connect dots between brief glimpses and vague impressions. But the collective weight of so many eerily similar accounts builds a foundation for the existence of an unknown North American primate finely adapted to wilderness survival.

As we scrutinize famous footage and biological evidence in later chapters, keep these reported behaviors and physical details in mind. They assemble into a cohesive picture of Bigfoot as intelligent, expert forest survivors lingering just at the edge of human perception. Science must expand its narrow definitions of reality to acknowledge the possibility of entire species that simply wish to be left alone in the few wild places remaining on this planet. For if we open our eyes, minds, and hearts, the wildmen in the woods may reveal themselves to us once more

So in summary

Physical Traits

- Height: 6-10 feet tall when standing upright
- Weight: 400-800 lbs
- Body hair: Entire body covered in hair from reddish brown to black
- Conical head: Bullet-shaped skull with no neck and minimal forehead
- Face: Human-like facial features with dark eyes, flat nose, and absence of prominent brow ridges
- Shoulders: Extremely broad and muscular upper body
- Arms: Overly long arms reaching down past knees
- Legs: Powerful muscular legs that enable bipedal walking
- Feet: Feet are up to 24 inches long and human-like but with arched instep

Behaviors

- Nocturnal activity patterns, most active at night
- Exceptional speed and agility moving through remote forests
- Leave oversized humanoid footprints measuring 16 inches or more
- Give off loud vocalizations including screams, howls, whoops, and wood knocks for communication
- React aggressively when startled, often bluff charging then veering away
- Show high intelligence by avoiding trail cameras and setting off traps without capture
- Mainly solitary but will gather in small family groups of 5-10 individuals

- Omnivorous diet including plants, berries, nuts, small animals
- Nomadic lifestyle, moving camp frequently, never staying in one area more than a few days
- Adept at climbing trees and swimming across lakes and rivers when needed
- Build crude stick nests on the forest floor for sleeping and shelter

Men or Ape

Based on sighting details and behavior, Bigfoot creatures seem to more closely resemble Gigantopithecus, an ancient 10 foot tall ape, rather than some primitive ancestral human like Neanderthals. While Bigfoot stands upright and has feet adapted for bipedal walking, key traits and actions appear more ape-like than human.

One of the most frequently reported behaviors is tree breaks, where Bigfoot creatures will twist tall saplings or snap thick tree branches, presumably as territorial sign posts or to vent frustration. Other great apes like gorillas and chimpanzees often perform similar dramatic displays of strength when confronting rivals. And the action requires grasping limbs with long arms and powerful hands, leveraging upper body strength over precision grip.

Related to tree breaks are the large, crude stick nests discovered in remote forests after sightings occur. Great apes build night nests on the ground by snapping and weaving together woody branches into a simple platform for sleeping. The nests attributed to Bigfoot closely resemble chimp or gorilla nest constructions rather than any human-made structure.

Intimidation displays offer more clues into ancient ape mannerisms. Numerous reports describe aggressive bluff charges where a Bigfoot will rush from the brush, snapping branches as it bellows aggressively then veers away at the last moment. Silverback gorillas commonly bluff charge to scare off intruders with an impressive display of speed, strength and fury prior to attacking. Even the loud vocalizations frequently described are more reminiscent of ape calls than human speech.

The physical form of Bigfoot also skews more toward a giant primate rather than any ancestor in the Homo genus. Features like the lack of neck, conical head that sits directly on the trapezius, flat nose with wide nostrils, and long arms with sloping shoulders match descriptions of Gigantopithecus rather than Neanderthal remains. And the full-body hair coat is distinctly primate, providing warmth and camouflage benefits in the forest consistent with modern apes.

Skeptics argue that upright walking makes Bigfoot seem more like primitive humans. But orangutans and certain chimpanzees will stand and stride bipedally when needed, especially when carrying food or objects across open spaces. Bigfoot may share this adaptation for short-range locomotion while retaining longer arms more suited for climbing than tool use. Their habitat lacks caves or cliffs that would drive bipedalism as seen in human ancestors.

Of course without an actual specimen, we cannot definitively classify Bigfoot as more ape than human. But cultural myths and eyewitness accounts overwhelmingly point toward a giant primate closely related to ancient apes that roamed North America until recently in evolutionary time. Their numbers likely dwindled with the spread of humans while modern science ignored all evidence of their existence. Only by embracing indigenous wisdom can we rediscover this lost cousin tragically driven to the brink.

Native Tales of the "Hairy Man"

Indigenous tribes have passed down stories of giant, wild "hairy men" in the forests of North America for countless generations, long before Europeans arrived. These rich oral traditions offer tantalizing clues into Sasquatch through Native eyes over the past 15,000 years. The accounts speak of powerful beasts that terrified witnesses, outsmarted hunters, and possessed supernatural talents that defied reality.

The Lummi tribe near the Canadian border tells of a time when all people lived underground near the river. But one restless boy wandered until he stumbled upon the Tsonoqua, the giant hairy wild woman gathering roots. She kindly offered to carry him, but he felt uneasy as she traveled faster than humanly possible through the deep woods. The boy ultimately escaped after leaving a trail for his uncle - a powerful shaman named Thunderbird - to follow by turning the trees red.

Perhaps the most revered Native artifact said to represent Sasquatch is a huge stone tablet kept by the Sts'Ailes Band near Harrison Lake in British Columbia. According to tribal history, the 300 pound red slate slab was authored by a powerful medicine man named Chee-ard to record his people's oral traditions before Christianization erased their culture. His pictographs specifically depict a giant, hairy wildman named sásq'ets that previously protected humans from threats until betrayal broke the trusting relationship.

Many tribes like the Sts'Ailes revere Sasquatch as benign forest guardians or teachers to guide shamans rather than fearsome monsters. But others recite chilling tales such as the account from California's Hoopa Valley, where a group of hunters found the mutilated remains of a prideful boy near a Bigfoot nest. The elders described 10-foot tall, foul-smelling beasts called Hairy Man who stalked the woods, feasting on human flesh during times of hunger and stealing children foolish enough to wander off alone.

Elders of the Nlaka'pamux in the Pacific Northwest's Fraser Canyon speak of the Scw'exmx, a race of wild mountain-dwelling creatures that would sneak into villages and steal dried salmon from food storage pits. But the Scw'exmx grew infuriated after a tribal member killed two cubs, bringing bloody retaliation where the beasts tore apart tipis and dragged away shrieking women during the night. Thereafter, the Scw'exmx avoided contact with humans at all costs except to take retribution on occasion.

Perhaps the most consistent theme across virtually all First Nation tribes is Sasquatch's preternatural ability to evade capture and disappear without leaving hard evidence of existence. The creatures seem to inhabit a liminal space between the material and spiritual worlds. The famous Lummi medicine man John Lame Deer claimed Native Americans descended directly from the Sasquatch tens of thousands of years ago. Over generations, the connection to nature faded as Native Americans developed language and culture while the Sasquatch continued roaming wild.

Deer described how tribal medicine men developed psychic abilities to communicate with their Sasquatch cousins across dimensions in order to gather information and request assistance. "They know how to go from one dimension to another," Lame Deer revealed. "They live in between...So it is possible for them to disappear in one place and reappear in another." This helps explain how the creatures seem to vanish inexplicably during sightings, defying efforts to collect proof.

The rich oral traditions spanning thousands of years suggest Sasquatch hold a special place in indigenous history as teachers, allies, and formidable wildmen to respect or avoid. They inhabited the land long before Native Americans or Europeans arrived, acting as supernatural guardians over the natural order. But betrayal, attacks, encroaching civilization, and environmental destruction eroded the trusting relationship over generations. Now the Sasquatch avoid contact out of self-preservation, watching from a dimensional veil as humanity destroys the sacred land they once protected together.

But across Native tribes scattered from coast to coast, the elders agree: Sasquatch still dwell among us as ghosts of the forest, materializing only to those deemed worthy for brief moments before retreating into the shadows. They are no mere animals, but beings that straddle cosmic planes, glimpsed only at the margins by humanity's limited senses. As one Sts'Ailes elder explained, "It lives in another dimension from us. But it can appear in this dimension whenever it has reason to."

To dismiss these stories as fanciful myths misses the deeper truth encoded within ancient wisdom. Indigenous tribes possessed a primal connection to the natural world lost to history. Their oral traditions reach back to the earliest memories of Turtle Island when mammoths roamed the land and North America teemed with megafauna. Native ancestors tread the same forests and mountains as Sasquatch for 15 millennia, observing, interacting, and passing down accounts to future generations.

While details shifted over time, the core descriptions of Sasquatch remained consistent no matter if the tribe dwelled in California, Alberta or Connecticut. All described giant hairy wildmen, 8-15 feet tall, that lived in remote woodlands and possessed an almost magical talent for avoiding human detection. And all warned these powerful creatures were not to be trifled with under any circumstances.

So perhaps it is time for science to set aside its narrow definitions of reality and listen to the wisdom of cultures that have interacted with these entities for thousands of years. Our ancestors knew of the "hairy giants" that left massive tracks and emitted chilling cries in the night. And those ancient wildmen still dwell among us, camouflaged just beyond the veil of perception, glimpsed only fleetingly as they have always been throughout the generations. We must open our minds to realities that defy our grasp...or risk losing the living ghosts of North America's primordial past.

Shocking Tales: Early Sightings by Settlers

Long before the famous Patterson-Gimlin footage in 1967, European explorers and pioneers documented perplexing accounts of encountering massive, hair-covered wildmen across the forests of North America for centuries. These bizarre stories from credible witnesses lent credence to Native tales of the Sasquatch, suggesting an actual unknown species awaited formal discovery.

As early as 1492, Christopher Columbus recorded in his ship's log an intriguing account from indigenous people describing fierce, hairy "wild men" that lived deep in the forests of the New World. Other early Spanish conquistadors told shocking tales of capturing bizarre-looking hairy giants roaming the woods that were slaughtered out of ignorance. The creatures were described as walking upright with ape-like features and a fierce resistance to capture.

One of the earliest documented sightings came from British explorer Samuel Hearne during his survey of northern Canada in 1799. While canoeing near the Coppermine River, Hearne wrote of spotting "an animal which my Indian companions called Math-e-thu." According to his guides, it was a fearsome hairy giant that stood as tall as a 6 foot man and left massive human-like tracks. Hearne wrote his "curiosity was much excited" by the unusual sighting.

Fast forward to the 1840s fur trapping era as American pioneers pushed west across the frontier. Tales of hairy wildmen began circulating around campfires from frightened trappers and astonished Indians. In 1847, a small party led by Caleb Lindahl fled Montana's Hell Roaring River with claims of being attacked by a band of huge creatures that threw rocks from cliffs with shocking strength and precision.

One early written account comes from 1850s miner Patrick Flaherty. While working his claim on Washington's Yakima River, Flaherty spotted a massive hair-covered beast drinking from the river that fled uphill after spotting the miner. Flaherty described it as an upright walking bear standing over 7 feet tall that left human-looking tracks. The unnerved miner packed up and abandoned his claim immediately thereafter.

But perhaps the most famous early sighting came in 1884 from British train engineers building the transcontinental railroad through remote British Columbia. Near Yale town, construction was halted by enormous humanoid tracks in the snow measuring 17 inches long. Soon after, multiple workmen reported seeing a dark hairy beast peering from behind trees that fled when approached. Fear spread rapidly, causing many crews to abandon tunneling efforts entirely.

Tales of the huge, foul-smelling beasts grew common enough during western expansion that newspapers began covering shocking stories. In 1893, the Daily British Colonist reported an enormous "Indian Devil" covered in long black hair that was spotted near Mount St. Lawrence in Victoria, BC. It reportedly had a horrific scream that terrified witnesses. Hunters formed multiple search parties but found nothing but large tracks.

Another early written account comes from 1918 in Washington's Mount St. Helens region. Prospector Fred Beck claimed that he and his mining crew were attacked one night by several rock-throwing ape-men that surrounded their cabin. The men shot at the beasts and discovered huge footprints the next morning. Similar stories emerged from other remote mining camps, attributing vandalism to bands of nocturnal hairy giants roaming the Cascades.

Over generations, enough credible sightings accumulated for Native tribes and frontiersmen to acknowledge that an unknown species of giant, hair-covered primate inhabited the dense forests of the Pacific Northwest and beyond. They became known as wild mountain devils, timber giants, or bushmen. But it was not until 1958 that newspaper articles coined the term "Bigfoot" to describe the elusive beasts based on enormous tracks found at a California logging site.

The stage was set for the famous Patterson-Gimlin footage that catapulted Bigfoot into mainstream consciousness in 1967. But for centuries prior, both indigenous tribes and pioneering explorers documented consistent accounts of intimidating hairy giants across North America that left behind massive footprints. Science simply ignored the shocking tales as superstitious fables or misidentifications. In reality, an unknown upright walking primate likely crossed paths with humanity since the earliest migrations across the Bering Strait land bridge.

The First Nations honored and feared Sasquatch as supernatural entities that guarded the sacred land. But the ignorance of settlers brought violence and death to the peaceful creatures, driving them deeper into remote sanctuaries. Now they retreat from any human contact, wanting no part of the civilizations encroaching upon their ancient forests. As old growth shrinks year by year, what few giants remain fade deeper into the shadows, perhaps vanishing entirely if we fail to act while proof still wanders the shrinking wilds of the continent its ancestors once dominated.+

Bigfoot Sightings Map

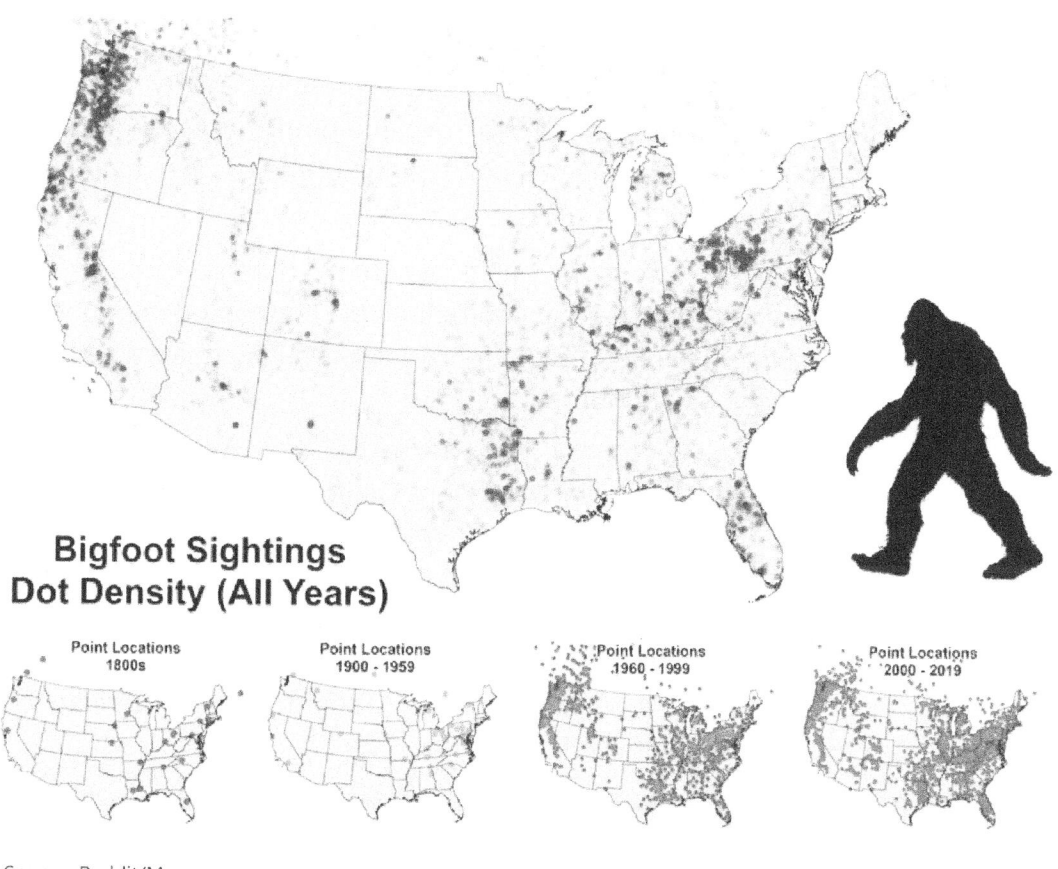

Source: Reddit/Mapporn

Where can I find Bigfoot

Bigfoot Hotspots of the Pacific Northwest

Spanning across the vast temperate rainforests of Northern California, Oregon, and Washington state, the Pacific Northwest has earned global fame as "Bigfoot Country" - the heartland of Sasquatch sightings and incidents. The remote habitat, with dense stands of old growth forest, secluded wilderness areas, and ample food sources, provides the ideal environment to sustain small populations of these elusive creatures hidden from civilization.

While sightings occur sporadically across the entire region, several areas stand out as particularly active hotspots where unusual concentrations of reports and intriguing evidence point to the possible existence of Bigfoot colonies dwelling deep within boundaries of protected park lands and forests.

Bigfoot Epicenter: The Legendary Habitat of Bluff Creek
Within the dense Six Rivers National Forest of Northern California, a remote gorge carved by Bluff Creek holds an almost mythic allure in cryptozoology circles. This tranquil wilderness basin comprising just a few square miles first gained fame in 1958 after road construction crews reported gigantic, mysterious footprints around their bulldozers and trailers after weekends off work. The news made international headlines as the "first Bigfoot evidence", though accounts of wild hairy giants roamed Native American lore for centuries prior across the Pacific Northwest.

When no Bigfoot sighting occurred in the wake of the tracks, interest soon faded. But nearly a decade later, Bluff Creek erupted onto the public imagination once again. Only this time, instead of footprints, a grainy 16mm film emerged purportedly showing a female Sasquatch walking along the creek bed. That explosive 24 seconds of footage galvanized generations of "squatchers" and launched the area into the pantheon of great cryptozoology sites.

In the over 50 years since the iconic Patterson-Gimlin film, the allure of Bluff Creek as prime Bigfoot habitat has only grown, attracting dedicated researchers and adventurers seeking their own encounter with the elusive beast that made the gorge famous.

Geography of a Bigfoot Hotspot

The Bluff Creek basin lies nestled between the snow-capped peaks of the Trinity Mountains range to the East and the lower Klamath Mountains of the Pacific Coast. The narrow valley follows the contours of Bluff Creek as it cascades down from alpine elevations above 5,000 feet before merging into the larger Klamath River drainage that runs to the sea.

The area sits squarely within the Klamath bioregion, characterized by a temperate rainforest climate, with wet winters and dry summers. The result is dense forests dominated by fir, pine, oak, madrone and redwood trees, with a rich ecosystem of salmon, deer, black bear and mountain lions - an ideal environment to sustain a large omnivorous primate year-round.

Bigfoot researchers describe key features that make the Bluff Creek habitat so suitable:

- Plentiful Food Sources - The creek and river provide salmon runs while the woodlands host berries, edible plants and plentiful small game.
- Abundant Fresh Water - The watershed offers clean water for drinking year-round - critical to survival.
- Prime Shelter Sites - Caves dot the granite cliffs lining the valley while thick stands of trees allow construction of nests and wind barriers.
- Low Human Presence - The remote gorge lacks major roads or development with few hikers or campers.
- Alluvial Soil - The loose creek soils hold fossils and tracks poorly explaining the dearth of bones or prints found.

The morning of October 20, 1967 dawned crisp and clear at Bluff Creek, California. Roger Patterson and Bob Gimlin were five days into their search for evidence of the elusive creature locals called "Bigfoot." Around midday, movement caught their eyes across the creek. Lumbering out of the forest came an imposing figure standing at least 7 feet tall with broad shoulders covered in glossy dark brown hair. the first film evidence lending credibility to Bigfoot reports, the footage brought public imagination to the possibility that an unknown North American ape roams our remote wildlands.

Revisiting the Patterson Film Site

Traveling along the overgrown logging roads still crisscrossing Bluff Creek, an adventurous squatcher can find the original site where Roger Patterson filmed his brief but sensational footage on October 20, 1967.

Following reports of massive tracks sighted earlier that year, Patterson and friend Bob Gimlin rode into the valley on horseback probing the dense woods. Rounding a bend in the creek, the pair spotted a large, hairy bipedal figure next to the water. Patterson quickly dismounted and managed to capture less than a minute of 16mm film as the figure glanced back at them then strode away into the forest.

The site remains largely unchanged save for the passage of time. The wide creek still ambles by over round stones under a canopy of tall pines and firs. The gravel bank where the creature walked away rises gently to the woods that conceal the path of its retreat. And near the water's edge lies a fallen tree on which to sit and imagine the thrill of that October day when two men and one Sasquatch collided briefly at this quiet corner.

Though Patterson died in 1972, Gimlin still recounts vivid details over 50 years later - the pungent odor permeating the area, deafening silence as wildlife sounds hushed, and their shared terror seeing an imposing "man-thing" alive in flesh rather than Native American lore. Yet the figure showed no aggression, merely turning to glance at them with apparent curiosity in her eyes.

That power of Bluff Creek endures - sustaining both the reality of all they encountered that afternoon as well as the visions of those still seeking their own connection with the unknown there.

Sporadic reports of Bigfoot encounters trickled out of Bluff Creek since the 19th century. But Patterson's film brought intense new interest that continues today. Within weeks of their iconic footage, the pair returned to cast massive tracks found miles upstream. And over subsequent years Patterson himself had multiple visual and audio sightings before his early death from cancer in '72.

Through the 1970s sightings increased, including a National Forest Service patrolman confronted by a large upright creature on a roadway along Bluff Creek. Hair samples found nearby underwent analysis showing an unusual protein profile.

By the 1980s, dedicated Bigfoot researchers began annual pilgrimages to monitor the valley, drawing headlines when loud nocturnal screams echoed from ridge tops. Others documented fresh 18-inch tracks found near creek. Some reported intense unease and rock throwing from hillsides. And huge nest-like constructions of pine boughs surfaced far from trails.

Recent decades show fewer high-profile incidents but consistent reports of campers hearing twig snaps and eerie calls at night, or stumbling onto massive prints along muddy banks. A few visitors each year still claim to glimpse figures bounding through the treeline across the creek. And so the legend of the valley's giant residents lives on half a century later.

Preserving the Sanctuary

Today Bluff Creek remains part of the protected Six Rivers National Forest, spared from development pressures. Redwoods loom over 300 feet tall along its ridges and the valley floor where dappled sunlight filters down. The area still lacks major roads, seeing only light foot traffic by anglers along its trout-filled waters.

And so this pristine refuge remains much as it was when Roger Patterson and Bob Gimlin rode through that autumn day in 1967, discovering that they were not alone. As witnesses to that iconic film scene pass on, new seekers inherit the landscape, listening for clues in the stillness of sunset. And the possibility lingers that around the next forested bend, another solitary figure waits to glance their way before vanishing upstream into the perpetual mystery that is Bluff Creek.

Sasquatch Capital of the Evergreen State: The Blue Mountains Habitat

The majestic Blue Mountains, spanning southeastern Washington and parts of northeast Oregon, remain one of the most active ongoing areas for Bigfoot encounters and evidence discoveries. Reports from this remote wilderness region - home to the famous Patterson-Gimlin film site - date back centuries in Native American legends. The high concentration of sightings, footprints, vocalizations and environmental traces make the Blues prime habitat for stealthy populations of the elusive hominid.

In this chapter we explore what makes the landscape so suitable, review milestone incidents that drove notoriety, and key areas that still draw intrepid squatchers hoping to glimpse the giant that roams the evergreen slopes.

Geography of a Bigfoot Hotspot

The Blue Mountain range spans over 10,000 square miles, bounded by the Snake River to the east and the Columbia River basin to the West. It consists of three distinct subranges stretching from the Wenaha-Tucannon Wilderness down across the Umatilla National Forest then south toward the Wallowa Mountains along the Oregon border.

The Blues contain classic Sasquatch terrain:

- Dense old growth and pine forests with limited roads or development
- Elevations up to 6,400 feet mixed with remote river valleys perfect for migration
- Minimal human population surrounded by miles of true wilderness beyond cell service
- Harsh winters drive wildlife to lower slopes with plentiful food and shelter

The area checks every box for sustaining small groups of reclusive primates, as demonstrated by over a century of persistent sightings.

Notable Sightings and Evidence Discovered

While Native tales mentioned "stick Indians" for ages, credible documentation began in 1920 when prospectors reported large tracks and strange whistling cries near their cabin. But events accelerated in 1968 just months after the Patterson film brought Bigfoot global fame. A sheriff's deputy responded to reports by high schoolers of a large upright beast rummaging their campsite near Walla Walla. Plaster casts were made of massive footprints before the stir faded.

In the 1970s accounts of skunk-like smells and unidentified calls came from remote homesteads. And the 1980s brought a wave of giant track finds - the most famous being 16-inch humanoid prints discovered repeatedly around Elk Wallow in the western Blues dubbed the "Cripplefoot tracks" for their abnormal gait patterns.

The 1990s proved most active, especially after local tobacco farmer Paul Freeman filmed a tall creature near Walla Walla in 1994. The controversial video showed a large Bigfoot walking a dry creek bed - similar to the creekbed backdrop in the Patterson footage. Though debunked by some, others assessed it as authentic, bringing waves of researchers to scour the region.

Recent decades see fewer high-profile incidents but consistent activity indicating the Blues remain prime habitat, with shelters and tracks found, plus accounts of rock throwing. And the 2000s saw new high-tech night vision and drone searches uncover large nest-like structures high in firs seeming to indicate seasonal migration habits.

Key Habitat Areas

Within the sprawling Blue Mountain complex, certain areas stand out for concentrations of encounters, supported by rich ecosystems capable of hiding small primate bands:

- The Mill Creek Watershed above Walla Walla where vast tracts of forest surround the creek and basin area where Freeman captured his disputed footage not far from where deputies cast prints in 1968.
- The Wenaha-Tucannon Wilderness spanning over 260,000 acres of raw untouched forest pocked with caves along the Oregon border. Its river valleys offer seasonal salmon runs critical for protein needs during winter months.
- The remote Grande Ronde River basin in the southeast quadrant, home to the famed "Cripplefoot" prints found near Elk Wallow. Its isolation and harsh winters discourage human activity.

Like similar Sasquatch terrains, the Blue Mountains offer ideal sanctuary. And while the high peaks see heavy snows that drive wildlife to lower elevations each winter, the dense primeval forests blanketing ridges and valleys allow migration access to food and shelter year-round - perfect for an intelligent species adapted to the cycles of the range.

And so legends continue of the giants that prowl the Blues. Not scattered transient migrants, but cunning beasts wise to the ways of their domain. Patient researchers still gather near campfires at night, listening for clues in the darkness. Ever hopeful the Blue Mountains' ghosts will reveal themselves once more.

The Volcano Habitat of Mount St. Helens

The dense temperate rainforests surrounding Washington state's iconic Mount St. Helens volcano represent prime Bigfoot habitat dating back nearly a century. Reports of giant "ape-men" lurking near mining claims first surfaced in 1924 when prospectors described being attacked by rock-throwing creatures in the remote gorge they dubbed "Ape Canyon". In the decades since, numerous sightings, vocalizations and environmental traces have originated along the mountain's slopes and around its foothills.

And while the catastrophic 1980 eruption decimated areas near the volcano, Bigfoot activity resumed soon after around the flanks of the peak. Today certain zones remain hotspots where hikers continue to report unnerving encounters with aggressive wildmen along the remote trails.

Notable Early Sightings:

While Native American lore referenced "mountain devils" for ages across the Cascades region, documented modern incidents began in the 1920s:

- July 1924 - Miners report repeated harassment by rock-throwing ape-men over several nights at their cabin near the base of the mountain they dubbed "Ape Canyon", describing a foul stench permeating the area.
- August 1967 – A local teacher captures film of an unidentified bipedal figure walking uphill from a distance considered by some to be a juvenile Sasquatch based on proportions.
- October 1969 – A group hunting elk describe a large, loud upright creature confronting and approaching their campsite near Meta Lake just months before the volcano's first stirrings.
- May 1980 - A father and son watch a large hair-covered biped cross Spirit Lake days before the catastrophic eruption, leaving tracks in the mud.

Bigfoot Habitat After the 1980 Eruption

When Mount St. Helens exploded on May 18, 1980 in the most significant eruption in modern times, the blast zone and pyroclastic flows sterilized over 230 square miles of forest. However within a few years, the areas outside the devastation zone saw animal and plant life recovering rapidly.

Reports of Bigfoot sightings soon resumed as well, especially on the eastern flanks in the foothills of the Mount Margaret Backcountry in the Gifford Pinchot National Forest, an area ripe with lakes, ponds and abundant wildlife.

Notable Sightings Since 1980

- 1993 – Cross-country runners describe a large upright hairy creature matching Bigfoot descriptions rapidly ascending a ridge near Coldwater Lake.
- 2005 – Hunters find peculiar large nest-like structures high in fir trees around Meta Lake constructed of bent and broken boughs, consistent with suspected Sasquatch shelters.
- 2012 – Mushroom pickers hear an unsettling high-pitched cry from ridge above them before rocks were thrown in their direction. They retreated quickly.
- 2021 – Hikers exploring Mount Margaret Backcountry report hearing intimidating wood knocks and vocalizations seeming to follow their group at a distance through the woods over several days.

Prime Habitat Zones

Research teams continue monitoring certain isolated zones around Mount St. Helens ideal for supporting small groups of reclusive hominids:

- The remote south flank of the volcano remains largely unexplored with extensive old growth forest, caves and secluded valleys perfect for concealment.
- The Mount Margaret Backcountry area encompassing dozens of lakes and abundant deer and elk to sustain year-round foraging, with very few roads or trails accessing thick woods.

- The upper Kalama River watershed spanning over 80,000 acres of raw rugged forest dotted with marshes and ponds, nearly all federally protected wilderness.

In addition, thermal imaging surveys have revealed heat signatures of possible wildlife retreats deep in steep terrain. And while not definitive, such anomalies intrigue Bigfoot investigators as to what may lurk unseen.

Much like other active volcanoes such as California's Mount Shasta, Mount St. Helens seems to possess an allure for Bigfoot as ideal habitat. And so legends and sightings persist of the mountain beasts adapted to life amongst the lava domes, craters and caves looming over the misty rainforest.

Epicenter of the Unknown: The Skookum Meadows Habitat

In the remote wilderness of Washington's Gifford Pinchot National Forest, a small clearing called Skookum Meadows holds an almost mythic allure in Bigfoot lore. Over the past 50 years, the nondescript area has produced hundreds of reported sightings and incidents hinting that a population of the giant cryptids may inhabit the dense temperate rainforest surrounding the meadows.

And in 2000, researchers uncovered a potential blockbuster piece of physical evidence – a huge 14-inch long depression in the mud appearing to show a large creature had laid down, with visible dermal ridges. The remarkable cast, dubbed the "Skookum Cast", made headlines around the world, cementing Skookum as a major hotspot for Sasquatch activity.

Geography of a Bigfoot Hotspot

Skookum Meadows spans less than a square mile but its location makes it prime real estate for sightings. Situated in the remote southeast corner of the Gifford Pinchot National Forest, it lies near the base of Pilot Rock, with no major roads or trails nearby. The clearing sits encircled by the towering old growth forests of the Cascades Mountain range, at an elevation of around 1500 feet. A minor creek tributary runs through the area, likely feeding into the larger Cowlitz River basin eventually.

The temperate rainforest ecosystem supports abundant food sources such as deer, elk, berries and edible vegetation. The mild, wet climate ensures year-round vegetation and drinking water as well. And the dense woods provide ample cover for nests or shelters. With no human development for dozens of miles, the meadows offer reliable isolation.

Key Sightings Through the Decades

Sporadic encounters likely occurred for decades before records began in the 1950s logging era. But incidents increased through the 60s and 70s:

- Campers reported heavy footsteps circling their tents at night accompanied by strange whistling sounds
- Bigfoot hunter Bob Titmus discovered large prints and heard odd vocalizations while staking out the area
- Hikers described a putrid stench permeating the meadows during mid-day
- Elk hunters saw a tall, upright hairy creature peering from behind a tree before retreating

The most famous occurrence came in 2000 when Bigfoot researchers investigating a rotting log noticed a huge 14-inch depression in the mud nearby, as if something large had laid down, plus a trail of similar tracks extending to the tree line. Their plaster cast of the print - later dubbed the Skookum Cast - revealed what appeared to be dermal ridges and hair imprints, causing a global sensation.

In recent years sightings continue of large, loud figures running through the meadows at dusk or lurking off trail. And reports persist of campers hearing wood knocks and unsettling howls echoing near their tents at night. The area remains a hotbed.

Why Skookum Meadows is Ideal Habitat

Several key features make the tiny Skookum Meadows so suitable for hosting a small community of reclusive Sasquatch:

- The remote location ensures minimal human activity with challenging access
- The surrounding old growth forest provides abundant shelter and foraging
- The meadow itself allows sky visibility for group gatherings or food gathering
- The mild climate enables year-round habitation without harsh winters
- The lack of roads facilitates safer migration to adjoining forest tracts

Of course the lack of roads also limits researchers hoping to deploy camera traps or DNA collection attempts. And the dense tree cover makes aerial thermal imaging difficult as well. Nevertheless, the area perfectly suits large primates seeking seclusion.

Much like the Patterson-Gimlin film site at Bluff Creek, the notoriety of Skookum Meadows endures decades later. And despite no definitive proof or captive specimen yet, the sheer volume of activity hints that something unknown inhabits that isolated forest niche. As one of the most active ongoing hotspots, Skookum Meadows holds clues waiting to be uncovered - perhaps by a future hiker brave enough to go off trail exploring for evidence of the elusive Sasquatch.

Bigfoot Hotspot: Salt Fork State Park

When most people think potential Bigfoot habitats, the dense Pacific Northwest forests come to mind or remote swamps of Florida. But unexpectedly, Salt Fork State Park in southeastern Ohio has rapidly gained notoriety as a Sasquatch sighting hotspot in recent years as expanding recreational land access has resulted in a wave of compelling reports from area campers, anglers, and hunters.

Tucked into the foothills of the Appalachian Mountains, Salt Fork attracts outdoors enthusiasts to its rolling woodlands dotted with lakes, streams, and hiking trails. And until the late 20th century, much of the nearly 20,000 acre preserve remained relatively undisturbed as primarily rugged backcountry where few ventured far from roads or campgrounds. But as facilities expanded, Salt Fork's mysterious wild residents began to reveal themselves.

As early as the 1980s, late night campers described hearing disturbing howls, knocks, and screams echoing from thickets surrounding their campsites. Large, loud bipedal creatures were sighted rummaging through coolers and ransacking poorly secured food bags after dark. Reports of 16-inch long humanoid tracks discovered along remote trails occasionally surfaced as well, peaking curiosity.

But Salt Fork's Bigfoot legend was cemented in 1994 when National Guard reservist Mark Matthews camped overnight with his wife, only to have their parked car shaken violently back and forth by a towering hairy creature in a display of aggression. Even eerier, Matthews managed to record a series of high-pitched wails on tape just before the creature retreated that primatologists could not identify with any known Ohio wildlife.

In the years since Matthews' frightening experience, Salt Fork sightings have steadily increased as more visitors explore further into remote sections only reachable by boat or backcountry trails. Reports range from loud vocalizations to massive fecal deposits discovered to campsite vandalism being blamed on the huge forest dwellers. The growing body of evidence suggests a small tribe of Bigfoots may inhabit pockets of Salt Fork's vast acreage.

The reasons for Salt Fork's unexpected popularity as a Bigfoot destination remain unclear, but the preserve features ideal habitat to conceal these elusive beasts. With over 150 miles of trails spanning massive old growth forests, swamplands, and meadows rich in edible flora, the park provides ample space for Bigfoots to roam relatively undisturbed. And generations of rare sightings indicate they have lurked in Ohio's eastern mountains long before recreation brought their domain creeping closer to civilization.

For now, Salt Fork retains its status as an intriguing modern hotspot attracting dedicated Bigfoot researchers seeking to finally bring the compelling evidence into mainstream recognition. And if legends hold true that an isolated tribe still roams the lonely Appalachian foothills, then Salt Fork's vast forests likely harbor them. The question remains - how much longer can the creatures avoid detection or will they further retreat from encroaching human boundaries? Either way, their days of living totally beyond belief seem numbered.

The Swamp Ape: Florida's Bigfoot

When one thinks potential Bigfoot habitat, the mental image invariably drifts to the great temperate rainforests of the Pacific Northwest or lonely snow-capped peaks of the Himalayas. But the American southeast, especially the sprawling marshlands of Florida, harbors its own surprisingly consistent history of giant, foul smelling wildmen known as the Skunk Ape lurking in remote wetland pockets.

While less famous than its northwest cousin, Florida's version closely parallels typical Bigfoot traits and behaviors. The bipedal creatures reportedly stand over 7 feet tall and walk upright on two legs. They are covered head to toe in shaggy hair and emit piercing cries. The beasts leave behind massive humanoid tracks and seem to display aggression when startled. Even eerie glow-in-the-dark eyeshine has been reported.

But the most notable divergence from northwest Bigfoot accounts lies in the creature's pungent odor, said to resemble rotten eggs or noxious skunk spray. This gives rise to the nickname Skunk Ape as witnesses universally describe an overpowering stench accompanying sightings. And the swamp-dwelling Skunk Ape seems specially adapted to traverse the humid, water-logged terrain that blankets much of Florida's interior where few humans dare tread.

The Seminole Tribe told early European settlers chilling tales of giant hairy wildmen named Esti Capcaki terrorizing remote wetland areas and feasting on human flesh when food grew scarce. Intriguingly, modern reported sightings closely align to these ancestral stories. Even famed Seminole leader Billy Bowlegs described a childhood encounter in the 1800s, further indicating a long history predating recent accounts.

In modern times, reports and traces emerge sporadically, centered in the sprawling Everglades and Big Cypress swamplands. A 2000 investigation discovered 16 inch barefoot tracks in dried mud showing dermal ridges, consistent with a 700 pound upright walker that matched no known wildlife. Campers report destroyed tent sites and piercing nocturnal screams echoing through the humid marshland darkness. Rangers even describe close encounters with the pungent beasts near secluded forest trails.

While evidence remains sparse and often anecdotal, Florida's remote swamplands seem ideal for small Skunk Ape tribes to silently dwell for generations. The road-less wetland expanses provide rich sources of edible plants while allowing the primates to traverse challenging terrain on two legs that would mire four-legged predators in the thick muck. And the consistently reported noxious odor offers evolutionary benefits for signaling territorial boundaries and discouraging close inspection by humans.

For now, the Skunk Ape remains relegated to cryptid status by mainstream science. But the persistent scattered accounts across Florida warrant deeper investigation. Evolution teaches that life adapts form to match unique environments. Perhaps in the case of Florida's fetid swamplands, an upright walking great ape variant managed to carve an isolated niche. If so, then a foul-smelling missing link may still haunt forgotten corners of the Sunshine State.

British Columbia's Habitats

While Washington and California soak up fame as Bigfoot homelands in the United States, Canada's westernmost province of British Columbia accounts for likely the highest concentration of Sasquatch reports and evidence discovered in North America.

Blanketed by over 600,000 square kilometers of raw untouched wilderness spanning towering coastal ranges, inland boreal forests and remote arctic tundra, British Columbia remains nearly as wild and untamed as when indigenous tribes like the Lil'wat and Secwepemc Nations told stories of the "Sasquatch" - meaning "wild man of the woods".

From early European explorers to modern witnesses, accounts persist of giant man-beasts lurking in one of Earth's last great wild frontiers where nature still rules supreme.

British Columbia's Habitats

95% of British Columbia's land mass remains undeveloped pristine wilderness. This spans diverse biomes perfect for concealment:

- The Coast Mountains spanning nearly 800 miles, with peaks over 15,000 feet and remote glacial valleys
- Ancient temperate rainforests with towering redcedars and spruce trees
- The northern Boreal forests of pine, fir, aspen and birch
- Rugged islands only accessible by boat or air
- The desolate subarctic tundra of the far north

The sheer scale and impenetrability provides endless hiding space for rare or unknown species. And First Nations peoples consider the legends as old as the land itself.

Early European Explorers Encounter Tales of "Wild Men"

When European fur traders like Alexander MacKenzie or Simon Fraser first penetrated British Columbia's interior in the early 1800s seeking beaver pelts and routes to the Pacific, indigenous trappers and villagers shared shocking accounts of giant wildmen stealing fish from stockpiles and leaving massive human-like footprints around remote camps.

The earliest settlers described hearing bone-chilling screams echoing from the darkness surrounding their isolated cabins and finding strange cylindrical stick structures unlike any made by Native tribes. Their diary entries indicate surprise but also acceptance that the endless forests likely harbored the unknown.

Reports Through the 20th Century

- In the 20th century, alleged encounters increased as remote mining and logging camps expanded into previously unexplored territories:
    - 1918 - A trapper reports shooting and wounding a large bipedal "mountain devil" trying to steal his sack near Pitt Lake. It screamed unlike any bear as it fled bleeding into the bush.
    - 1924 – Nightwatchmen at a Vancouver Island mining operation report being stalked by large rock throwing assailants over several evenings that emitted a stench unlike any known wildlife.
    - 1958 – A lumberjack documents finding 18-inch human-like tracks in a remote valley near Bella Coola leading into a crude stick shelter structure.

By the 1950s the number of documented sightings by remote work crews climbed rapidly, making headlines in local papers. The most famous incident came in 1967 when road construction supervisor Albert Ostman claimed to be abducted by a family of Sasquatch while prospecting near Toba Inlet, describing them as intelligent, social creatures that communicated with each other. His detailed account only brought more interest and witnesses emerging.

Hotspot Regions

While sightings occur province-wide, certain zones stand out for higher concentrations of activity and prime habitat capable of sustaining small Bigfoot family clans:

- The Fraser Valley from Vancouver east through the Coast Mountains where the famous 1967 Patterson-Gimlin film originated near Bluff Creek in California - considered an extension of the same forest ecosystem and watersheds.
- Vancouver Island, with over 12,000 reported incidents, including the 1924 sighting by miners of rock throwing "mountain devils"
- The Interior Plateau region, where the earliest indigenous tales originated near villages around Kamloops and Jasper.
- The vast Great Bear Rainforest blanketing the province's northwestern coastal fjords and inlets - one of the largest intact temperate rainforests left on Earth.

And so in the vastness of British Columbia, reports continue from remote camps and rural homesteads convincing many that the Sasquatch still roams as it has for ages - a stealthy guardian of the forests avoiding human contact as civilization encroaches on their domain. But for now, the endless mountains, valleys and thick woods still offer sanctuary.

When Giants Attack: The Harrison Hot Springs Habitat

Within the dense forests blanketing the region around Harrison Lake in southwestern British Columbia, the scenic village of Harrison Hot Springs holds a notorious place in Sasquatch lore. Now a tourist destination known for its natural hot spring resort, in the 1940s Harrison became site of the explosive "Chief Loolaas Monster" incident, when an abusive Bigfoot reportedly emerged to pelt the settlement with rocks after crews began clearing its habitat. The story made headlines as crews even dynamited a cave said to be the creature's lair before sightings ceased. But Harrison Hot Springs remains known for Bigfoot activity even today.

The Harrison Lake Region

Harrison Hot Springs sits on the southern shores of long, deep Harrison Lake, surrounded by the thick Douglas fir and cedar forests of the Pacific Coast Mountain range. Like nearby Agassiz, it started as a farming and logging town after European settlement began in the mid-1800s. And just five miles south lies the Harrison River, running down from the mountains through Sasquatch Provincial Park, named for reported sightings as early as the 1880s by loggers and trappers.

The dense woods allowed communities to spring up in isolation. But their very remoteness soon allegedly brought conflict with the regions' most famous cryptid inhabitant - the Chief Loolaas Monster itself.

The Chief Loolaas Incident
According to local history, settlers had reported hearing strange cries echoing from certain caves and alcoves around Harrison Lake since the late 1800s. But they assumed the noises belonged to bears. By the 1940s, Harrison Hot Springs began drawing tourists to

its newly discovered natural mineral hot springs, allowing construction of hotels and commercial lodges.

In March 1948 as crews cleared land to expand resort facilities, a barrage of heavy rocks began bombarding homes and vehicles near construction zones at night. Windows shattered and cars dented as if under deliberate attack. Terrified residents reported hearing guttural screaming emanating from the forests during the attacks. Some even described a towering, hair-covered creature glimpsed squatting atop a rocky outcrop.

When attacks continued over several weeks, a notorious local hunter named Bill Roe was dispatched to kill the "devil" said by elders to be Chief Loolaas, known in native myth as the "Wild Man of the Woods". Roe soon located a cave along the lakeshore littered with bones and excrement with a putrid smell, surmising it as the beast's lair. After dynamiting the cave, the assaults ceased, leading to theories the creature had fled or been killed. Cryptozoologists speculate the explosive encroachment on its territory prompted the violent defensive response.

Modern Sightings

In subsequent decades sightings have continued, if less dramatic, throughout the region:

- Hikers describe finding massive humanoid tracks along remote trails
- Campers report strange howls seeming to answer their calls at night
- Hunters reveal finding peculiar branch structures and giant nests deep in the backcountry
- Drivers claim sighting tall, upright fur-covered figures that cross forest roads and disappear

While many sightings surely remain unreported, the area's history and habitat make it prime ground for stealthy creatures. And the Chief Loolaas legend lives on. Perhaps a new generation of tourists will have their own close encounter while soaking in the hot springs outside town.

Epicenter of Encounters: The Fraser Canyon Habitat

Winding over 180 miles through the rugged Coast Mountains of south-central British Columbia, the plunging Fraser Canyon follows the swift waters of the Fraser River past towering cliffs and dense cedar and fir forests that obscure remote side valleys. This largely roadless landscape has accumulated alleged Bigfoot accounts for over a century - from pioneer tales to Native legends.

The area holds special notoriety in Sasquatch lore as home to the famous 1924 claim by prospector Albert Ostman that he was abducted and held captive by a family group of the creatures for nearly a week in a hidden valley. The detailed story brought the first widespread attention to British Columbia as prime habitat for these elusive beasts. Encounters persist to current times from campers, loggers and miners spending days along the Fraser's lonely lengths.

Notable Sightings Through the Years

Fur trappers were likely the first Europeans to record surprise at Native tales of the Sasquatch, but prospectors and railway crews soon reported their own bizarre encounters:

- Late 1800s - Chinese railway workers describe harassment by rock-throwing "mountain men" near construction camps.
- Early 1900s – Trappers recount finding huge crude shelters and giant footprints along secluded riverside beaches usually containing salmon.
- 1924 – Prospector Albert Ostman shares detailed account of being abducted by a family group of Sasquatch for nearly a week before escaping.
- 1940s – Railway crews detail incidents of strange unidentified creatures witnessed stealing fish from storage sheds along the tracks.
- 21st century – Modern campers and canoeists continue seeing giant barefoot tracks and destroyed campsites with food stolen.

Why The Canyon Offers Ideal Habitat

The Fraser Canyon environment contains every element needed to conceal small populations of rare hominids:

- Heavy tree canopy covering steep slopes to obscure views
- An abundance of salmon and wild game to supply year-round sustenance
- Caves and secluded side valleys perfect for shelter sites
- Harsh winters that discourage human activity
- Minimal roads or settlements across vast distances

Much like Washington's Columbia River Gorge just south of the border, the Fraser Canyon appears purpose-built as a sanctuary for stealthy giants.

And so in the thriving darkness of its forests, big secrets may still lurk. Modern witnesses to torn tents and mammoth tracks keep alive what trappers and tribes knew for ages - this landscape remains domain of the unknown. And the swatch of hairy creatures said to guard its lonely lengths show themselves only when they choose. But their traces suggest they still walk here in the shadows.

Prince George Region

Considered British Columbia's capital of Sasquatch sightings, the area near Prince George has generated hundreds of reports, including William Roe's famous 1955 close encounter and the Ruby Creek mining attack in 1941 said to have left several miners dead and injured by rock-hurling beasts. The region remains very active today.

In the end, with so much undisturbed wilderness still dominating the province, British Columbia seems poised to produce even more world-class evidence of these elusive giants that its indigenous people honored for millennia before Europeans brought violence and dismissal. Perhaps by at last acknowledging the ubiquitous Native accounts, today's Canadians can write the next chapter of discovery by embracing what still wanders the endless forests outside their cities.

Alberta's Overlooked Sasquatch Accounts

When one considers potential Bigfoot habitat, the towering old growth rainforests of British Columbia immediately south or the legendary Pacific Northwest forests further beyond come to mind. But Canada's prairie province of Alberta offers its own surprisingly consistent history of Sasquatch accounts that suggest the territory's ample remote wilderness also sustains these reclusive creatures.

Alberta spans over 255,000 square miles, much of it dominated by the eastern front of the Canadian Rockies which rise sharply from the central plains. These imposing, largely impassable mountains harbor thick stands of pine, spruce and fir forest peppered with alpine meadows, limestone caves, and abundant wildlife sustenance to support a small population of elusive primates. And for centuries, scattered sightings have surfaced from across this daunting landscape.

The Stoney Nakota First Nations told early European fur traders chilling tales of the wild hairy giants named Chiye Tanko who walked like men and dwelled deep in the remotest peaks and valleys of what is now Banff and Jasper National Parks. Even the earliest pioneer accounts described disturbing encounters with foul-smelling wildmen and discovery of massive humanoid tracks across isolated mountain traplines.

In modern times, a database of over 400 Alberta Sasquatch reports spans the province's forested mountain terrain. Compelling cases include a 1988 incident where seismic surveyors discovered 17-inch long humanoid tracks in a remote pass that followed them for miles before veering away. Hunter reports range from huge manlike beasts paralleling them to discovering unidentified primate remains partially buried. And a 2018 report told of a large auburn-haired creature throwing stones at a cabin near Abraham Lake before screams sent the witnesses fleeing in terror.

While much reporting focuses on British Columbia as Canada's Sasquatch capital, Alberta's equally remote boreal and subalpine forests likely harbor a similar percentage of sightings that never get officially documented by authorities. And generations of accounts passed down by both indigenous tribes and frontiersmen indicate these elusive giants have lurked in the region's most secluded peaks and thickets for centuries.

Perhaps by finally acknowledging the rich cultural history and modern sighting data, Alberta can shed outdated perceptions as merely a flatland prairie province. For within its rugged backbone of imposing Rockies granite, the wild giants of the mountains still walk where few have dared tread. And if we listen closely to ancestral wisdom, their calls still echo from the shadows.

Sasquatch Capital of Eastern Canada: Northern Ontario's Overlooked Habitats

When one considers potential Bigfoot habitat, the towering ancient rainforests of British Columbia's Pacific coast or the high peaks of the Washington Cascades first come to mind. But Canada's largest province Ontario has produced a surprisingly robust history of Sasquatch accounts across its remote central and northern forests rivaling its western counterparts.

While southern Ontario faces heavy development and urbanization around Toronto, the central and especially northern sections still contain vast spans of raw boreal forest and wetlands nearly as pristine as centuries ago. Both indigenous oral traditions and contemporary sighting reports suggest this challenging habitat conceals small tribes of elusive Sasquatch.

Ontario's Remote Wilderness

Northern Ontario spans over 415,000 square miles blanketed primarily by boreal forest with thousands of lakes and rivers. The subarctic climate brings harsh winters with heavy snowfall that discourages travel or settlement across much of this landscape. It remains nearly as untamed as when Algonquin, Ojibwe and Cree tribes passed down stories of the "Wendigo" - giant wildmen stalking hunters through the endless woods.

Even French fur traders and missionaries wrote disturbing accounts from remote outposts of gigantic humanoid tracks discovered around their camps. And into modern times, a consistent chronicle of "wild mountain devils" has endured from trappers, loggers and adventurers braving the endless forests.

A Database of Sightings

- In recent decades, a catalog of over 300 credible Ontario Sasquatch sightings has emerged, primarily concentrated north of Lake Nipissing towards James Bay where the remoteness provides ideal cover. While many sightings surely go unreported across the vast terrain, recorded accounts include:
    - Campers witnessing large bipedal figures watching their campsites from the forest edge
    - Hunters describing being followed for miles by unseen giants paralleling their path
    - Hikers finding massive, barefoot humanoid tracks deep in protected parks
    - Wildlife officers discovering strange branch and rock structures unlike any indigenous ones

While most evidence proves circumstantial, the consistency across centuries begs the question what exactly are these remote woodsmen encountering in the dark northern forests?

Why Northern Ontario Offers Ideal Habitat

Northern Ontario contains every condition necessary to conceal small populations of rare hominids:

- Over 80% of the land is dense boreal forest perfect for concealment from humans
- Harsh, snowbound winters that keep intrusion by settlers or industry limited
- An abundance of lakes, rivers, and woodland game to supply year-round sustenance
- Caves and secluded valleys that allow shelter from the elements
- Limited road access across the endless wooded tracts

In essence, northern Ontario harbors the perfect habitat for Sasquatch to remain hidden indefinitely. And while western Canada grabs headlines, this eastern land of lakes and forests warrants closer inspection by serious cryptozoologists as a potential hotspot. The rich cultural history paired with growing modern sightings suggest robust ecosystems still exist to sustain small bands of these elusive giants. And until thorough investigations sweep these remote woodlands, the wild specters of past and present tales still beckon the daring to unravel their mystery once and for all.

Alaska's Overlooked Wildmen: The Panhandle's Prime Habitat

When one pictures an ideal Bigfoot habitat, the mental image inevitably wanders to the moss-draped cedar forests of Washington and British Columbia. But Alaska's southeastern Panhandle region offers equally prime refuge for Sasquatch - an overlooked temperate rainforest wilderness cloaked in mystery and forgotten lore.

The Panhandle Coast

Alaska's Panhandle constitutes the 500-mile long, narrow southeastern spur wedged between British Columbia and the Gulf of Alaska. Heavily glaciated rugged peaks of the Coast Mountains plunge into a tangled archipelago of forested islands dotting the Alexander Archipelago stretching north towards Juneau. It remains one of Earth's last intact temperate rainforest ecosystems.

The region still relies heavily on fishing, mining and logging supporting small towns and villages accessible often only by boat or seaplane. Beyond these isolated outposts sprawl endless tracts of virgin forest where man has barely tread. In essence, ideal terrain for legends like the Sasquatch to avoid detection indefinitely.

Native Tales and Early Accounts

The Tlingit and Haida peoples native to the Panhandle passed down oral traditions for ages regarding large hairy "wood giants" that dwelled deep in the ancient forests. When Russian fur traders arrived in the mid-1800s, they too reported hearing strange cries echoing across the mountains at night around their remote trapping cabins.

Over the decades, frontiersmen prospecting mines or cutting timber brought back bizarre accounts from the backcountry of gigantic tracks by streams, huge logjams pulled down by some powerful force, and eerie screams that caused sled dogs to cower in fear. The endless woods held secrets the indigenous tribes accepted as part of their reality.

Modern Sightings and Evidence

In recent decades, alleged encounters continue, especially as remote logging roads push deeper into untrammeled valleys and ridges:

- Bear hunters describe large rocks and logs thrown towards their camps with no origin point visible.
- Hikers recount coming across massive shelters constructed from entire tree trunks stacked 20 feet tall in areas far from any human presence.
- Kayakers witness tall, bipedal reddish-brown creatures watching them from shoreline bluffs before bounding into the forest as they approach for a better look.
- Prospectors uncover 19-inch barefoot prints high in alpine passes far from established trails.

And so in the enigmatic wilderness straddling the border between Washington and British Columbia's forests, the wandering giants remain. Their reported traces suggest the species still roams as it did when Native hunters tracked woolly mammoths past glaciers across the land bridge from Asia so long ago. Perhaps science will yet connect the dots between the elusive strands of evidence scattered across an overlooked land where mystery still reigns in the endless rainforest.

Alaska's Forgotten Wildmen: The Interior's Prime Habitat

When one considers potential Bigfoot habitat, the mental image invariably wanders to the moss-draped cedar rainforests of Washington and British Columbia. But the remote boreal woodlands and soaring peaks of Alaska's little known interior contain equally prime refuge for small tribes of these elusive giants forgotten to time.

The Alaskan Interior Wilderness

While coastal Alaska accounts for a rich history of Sasquatch accounts from Tlingit and Haida tribes near sea level, the harsher interior spanning over 400,000 remote square miles contains barely a single paved road, allowing a rugged expanse for such creatures to roam hidden from humanity.

Encompassing boreal taiga forest, sprawling arctic tundra and the towering Brooks Range slicing the state nearly to Canada, Alaska's interior remains nearly as untamed as centuries past. It may be the last true wilderness left on the continent where mammoths once roamed.

Native Tales and Early Accounts

Athabaskan tribes like the Gwich'in and Tanana have occupied the remote interior for over 10,000 years, subsisting as nomadic hunters and fishermen. Their oral traditions contain references to "wood giants" and "stick Indians" inhabiting the dense forests and high valleys.

Russian fur traders reported hearing strange screams at night from unseen beasts while canoeing the Yukon River watershed. Gold prospectors flooded the region in the 1800s chasing rumors of riches, but many fled describing giant "wild men" harassing their camps. By the early 20th century few whites had witnessed or mapped much of Alaska's core beyond the Yukon River.

Modern Sightings & Evidence

In the last half century, alleged encounters increased as air travel improved access to remote areas:

- Trappers describe massive logjams pulled down by some powerful force on the Tanana River near Fairbanks far from any roads or settlements.
- Air taxi pilots report flyovers of extremely tall, hair-covered bipeds walking upright along frozen riverbeds miles from the nearest village.
- Caribou hunters reveal finding peculiar large nest structures built between trees and hillsides presumably to escape arctic winds.
- Seismologists working near the Brooks Range describe intimidating wood knocks and rock throwing around their campsites at night though no bears or humans were visibly present in the barren landscape.

While many accounts no doubt go unreported across the vast terrain, the consistency of description around a certain type of rare creature raises eyebrows. And with 95% of the Alaskan interior devoid of any permanent human presence, the habitat surely remains for populations of Sasquatch to still roam free as their ancestors did over the land bridge eons ago when glaciers still dominated the peaks. Perhaps in time, science will catch up with Native wisdom to acknowledge the wildmen still walking here.

What Sasquatch Eats

The diet of Bigfoot, much like the creature itself, is shrouded in mystery and speculation. As an alleged large, bipedal hominid, Bigfoot is often theorized to be omnivorous, much like humans and other primates. This chapter will delve into the potential dietary habits of Bigfoot and explore the correlation between these habits and the reported locations of sightings.

Firstly, let's consider the Pacific Northwest, a region with a high concentration of Bigfoot sightings. This area is rich in resources, with a diverse array of plant and animal life. If Bigfoot is indeed an omnivore, it would have a wide variety of food sources to choose from. Berries, nuts, and roots are abundant in these forests, as are deer, elk, and smaller mammals. The rivers teem with fish, particularly during the salmon runs, which could provide a high-protein food source.

Reports of Bigfoot-like creatures in the Rocky Mountains suggest a diet adapted to this rugged environment. The alpine and subalpine ecosystems are home to large ungulates such as elk, mule deer, and bighorn sheep, which could serve as potential prey. Additionally, the region's rivers and lakes offer fish, while the forests and meadows provide a variety of plant life, including berries, nuts, and tubers.

In the Great Lakes region, the mixed forests and freshwater ecosystems could support a Bigfoot population with a diverse diet. The area's waterways are rich in fish, while the surrounding forests offer a variety of fruits, nuts, and vegetation. The region is also home to a variety of game, including deer, rabbits, and birds.

In the southern swamplands and subtropical forests, a Bigfoot creature would have access to a different set of resources. Fish, shellfish, and amphibians are plentiful in these wetlands, as are wild hogs, alligators, and a variety of bird species. The dense vegetation also provides a variety of fruits, nuts, and roots.

The correlation between these reported Bigfoot habitats and the creature's potential diet is intriguing. Each region offers a unique set of resources that could sustain a large omnivorous creature. The diversity of these diets could also explain the wide range of Bigfoot descriptions and behaviors reported in different areas.

However, it's important to note that a creature the size of Bigfoot would require a significant amount of food. This raises questions about the ecological impact of a Bigfoot population. For instance, a large predator or omnivore could potentially disrupt local ecosystems by overhunting or over-foraging. Yet, there is little definitive evidence of such disruptions, which adds another layer of mystery to the Bigfoot enigma.

Furthermore, the scarcity of Bigfoot sightings could suggest a low population density, perhaps due to a large home range or a solitary lifestyle. This could help explain why Bigfoot remains elusive despite its purported size and diet.

In conclusion, the potential diet of Bigfoot, based on the resources available in reported sighting locations, paints a picture of a versatile omnivore capable of adapting to a variety of environments. However, the lack of concrete evidence leaves much of this picture to speculation. As we continue to explore the mystery of Bigfoot, the creature's diet and its correlation with sighting locations offer intriguing avenues for further investigation.

Migration Theories

The distribution of Bigfoot sightings has long intrigued investigators. Encounters seem to concentrate in regional pockets, then mysteriously vanish for years before flaring up again hundreds of miles away. This elusive movement pattern suggests nomadic creatures periodically migrating through areas rich in seasonal food sources and shelter. Their remoteness and wariness means we only catch fleeting glimpses as they traverse their territories. Some researchers plot sightings geographically and theorize likely migration routes that follow waterways, ridgelines, game trails and forest cover.

One hypothesized route traces from the Fraser River region of British Columbia south through the Cascades range along the Columbia River system down through Oregon and Northern California. The Sierra Nevada mountain forests offer habitat continuity allowing further dispersal south through the Southwest. A Midwest route theorizes migration from northern Minnesota through the Great Lakes region and into the Ohio River valley. In the east, a route theorized from the forests of Maine southwesterly follows the Appalachians through the mid-Atlantic states. Meanwhile, the swamps and everglades of Florida harbor a resident population theorized to be the Skunk Ape.

Seasonal migration may move these highly mobile hominids hundreds of miles along traditional paths. Summer in northern climates offers plentiful forage, while winters prompt southern shifts to milder climates with sustenance still available. These seasonal migration corridors likely follow remote mountain chains, forest networks, river systems and watershed ridges that allow concealment and access to food year-round. In the spring and fall, eyewitness flurries occur during transition periods when Sasquatches are on the move.

Their territories require vast land ranges spanning thousands of square miles. Family units likely stake out forested zones in home ranges while juveniles roam further afield seeking their own habitats, accounting for more dispersed sightings of young bachelor Bigfoots in odd locations. Canadian reports indicate possible north-south seasonal migration as well, avoiding bitterly cold winters. Nomadic by nature, migration patterns remain unpredictable but allow the species as a whole to exploit resources across the continent.

Bigfoot worldwide

Yeti

The Yeti, also known as the Abominable Snowman, is one of the most famous cryptids in the world. For centuries, people indigenous to the Himalayas have told tales of a large, hairy, bipedal creature that lives among the snowy peaks. The name "Yeti" comes from the Tibetan word "Yeh-teh" which translates to "little man of the snows." Though no conclusive evidence has surfaced proving the Yeti's existence, its legend continues to capture the imagination of adventurers and cryptozoologists alike.

Descriptions of the Yeti vary, but some common characteristics emerge. It is typically described as standing nearly 8 feet tall when upright on two legs and weighing over 300 pounds. Its entire body is covered in long, shaggy hair that ranges in color from reddish-brown to nearly white. Large footprints measuring up to 24 inches long have been attributed to the Yeti, along with unearthly calls and whistles carrying through the frigid mountain air. Some Himalayan people consider the Yeti to be a dangerous predator, while others believe it possesses magical powers or sees it as a sacred entity.

The Yeti is said to inhabit the snowy, unforgiving landscape of the Himalayas year-round, venturing across Nepal, Tibet, and the mountainous region where India, China and Bhutan intersect. It makes its home in remote caves and survives on available food sources like mountain goats, rodents, and berries. Though the Himalayan mountains only average 30 degrees Fahrenheit, the Yeti's thick fur coat allows it to thrive. Reports of Yeti sightings occur frequently on the Tibetan Plateau and surrounding peaks over 15,000 feet high. Mount Everest, Annapurna, and Makalu are rumored hotspots.

The first documented Western sighting of mysterious large footprints speculated to belong to the Yeti dates back to 1889, when Major L.A. Waddell discovered them during an expedition. As the 20th century saw more adventurers drawn to scale the Himalayan peaks, stories and evidence of the Yeti became more widespread. In 1921, a journalist photographed strange prints in the snow and large creatures moving in the distance. Over the next few decades, climbers began reporting unsettling howls echoing off the mountains and colossal footprints traversing their paths.

Perhaps the most famous piece of evidence surrounding the Yeti is a collection of photographs taken by British explorer Eric Shipton in 1951 on the Menlung Glacier between Tibet and Nepal. The pictures show a distinct trail of human-like footprints crossing the snowfield. Though several scientists judged them inconclusive at the time, the Shipton photographs sparked global curiosity. Soon Yeti-hunting expeditions were mounting with hopes of capturing the elusive beast.

In 1953 Sir Edmund Hillary, the first man to summit Mt. Everest, searched for evidence of the Yeti during his expedition. Though unsuccessful, his interest fueled further investigation into the cryptid. Over the next few decades, various organizations like the World Book Encyclopedia and the Smithsonian sponsored trips to search for the Yeti. They employed infrared cameras, motion detectors, DNA analysis and more in attempts to validate its existence with concrete proof. Though these expeditions added to the pool of eyewitness testimonies and footprint castings, they were largely unable to prove the Yeti exists as a real creature.

Skeptics largely dismiss the Yeti as local superstition, legend, or misidentification of known animals like bears or langur monkeys. They claim evidence like footprints are too difficult to authenticate in remote terrain and often turn out to be naturally-occurring marks or hoaxes. Believers counter that the Yeti still roams the wildest, most untouched corners of the Himalayan landscape much of which has yet to be explored by man. Enough eyewitness accounts and trace evidence exist to warrant further scientific investigation, they claim.

Today, the Abominable Snowman remains one of the most popular cryptids investigated by cryptozoologists around the world. Expeditions searching for proof of the Yeti's existence continue today, though frequently impeded by the extreme Himalayan conditions. Advancements in technologies like DNA analysis offer new hope of one day finding evidence to solve the centuries-long mystery. Until then, the Yeti retains its legendary status as the elusive protector of the world's highest peaks, capturing adventurers' wonder about what still lurks at the top of the world.

China's Elusive Wildman

Deep in the remote high-altitude woodlands of central and southern China dwells a rare creature locals call Yeren - the "wildman." Eyewitness and track reports spanning decades paint a consistent portrait of a six to eight foot tall, bipedal, hair-covered hominoid that flees human contact. But brief glimpses and chance encounters tell tantalizing stories of its existence.

These elusive forest dwellers resemble other global "wildmen" like the Yeti and Bigfoot. Chinese researchers speculate the Yeren may be a remnant population of Gigantopithecus - an extinct ten-foot-tall ape - or possibly even a new primate species unknown to science. But despite decades of alleged sightings and habitat studies, definitive proof remains lacking. Like all great woodland mysteries, the Chinese wildman refuses either confirmation or extinction.

A Red-Haired Relic Ape in Remote Forests

Modern Yeren accounts first surfaced widely in remote Shennongjia forest of Hubei province in the 1970's. State forestry departments sent investigative teams who recorded over 100 eyewitness interviews and made plaster casts of odd, large footprints. These 15-inch tracks with prominent big toes didn't match any known Chinese wildlife. Locals described a foul-smelling, red-furred, humanlike beast standing up to ten feet tall and emitting piercing nocturnal shrieks.

Government researchers speculated Gigantopithecus survival as the most plausible explanation. This extinct giant ape, known from fossil mandibles and teeth across Asia, roamed China until about 300,000 years ago. If rare Yeren sightings describe reality, a relic population somehow endured undiscovered in China's vast remote woodlands.

The Chinese Academy of Sciences took the possibility seriously enough to establish the China Yeren Research Center in Shennongjia. Their scientists continue investigating the mystery today alongside global cryptozoologists. And over the decades, intriguing stories and encounters have added to the mystery of China's elusive wildman.

Memorable Yeren Encounters

A Red-Haired Female and Child

In 1980, forestry worker Luo Baosheng reported spotting a reddish-brown, female Yeren accompanied by a smaller child-like Yeren near Mowei Reservoir. The creatures foraged for fruit in the brush until detecting Luo's presence after several minutes. They immediately fled on two legs deeper into the forest. The smaller one ran with an odd bent-knee gait that convinced Luo he had witnessed relic survivors of a rare primate.

A Ten-Foot Giant Crossing a River

In 1991, local businessman Bu Xiaoqiu observed an incredible sight while fishing near a remote mountain river. A massive, ten-foot-tall, reddish-brown Yeren waded across the river just dozens of feet away. It had a small flat face with wide mouth and head that sat directly atop its shoulders with no neck. The giant wildman took over a minute to splash slowly across, giving Bu an astounding clear look. Though China's forestry department investigated extensively, no further trace turned up.

A Nighttime Roadside Encounter

Driving home late one evening in 2009, businessman Su Changjin slammed his brakes as an immense dark shape lumbered across the road near Shuitangba. Stopping to avoid hitting what he thought was a bear, Su was shocked when his headlights illuminated a powerfully built Yeren frozen in mid-stride. It stood well over seven feet tall, covered in reddish-brown hair except for its face. Su made direct eye contact with the creature before it dashed into the bordering yellowwood forest. He noted an overpowering stench like rotting garbage lingering after its sudden departure.

A Hunter's Daytime Sighting

Out hunting mushrooms in remote Wulong Mountain forest one autumn afternoon in 2015, Zheng Weixing heard his dogs' excited barking as they chased something large through the brush. Expecting a deer or boar, Zheng was stunned when he caught sight of them pursuing a six-foot-tall, reddish-brown Yeren running powerfully on two legs. It crashed ahead of the dogs through dense undergrowth with ease for about 20 seconds before vanishing from view. Zheng's dogs refused to follow the wildman any further into the woodlands.

Night Watchman's Shocking Encounter

A Shennongjia forest night watchman named Wu was patrolling a remote mountain road one midnight in 2020 when a rock struck his patrol jeep hard enough to dent metal. Shining his flashlight toward the steep slope it had tumbled from, Wu was shocked to briefly spot a muscular, eight-foot-tall, red-furred Yeren glaring back down at him. It emitted a deep roar that echoed through the mountains before turning to bound easily up the 60-degree precipitous ridge into darkness. Wu noted its fluid agility moving faster than any human possibly could among the cliffs. He speculated it had deliberately thrown the rock to halt his vehicle.

These and similar bizarre stories from serious eyewitnesses keep the Chinese wildman mystery alive. While most Western scientists dismiss the Yeren as imagination or mistaken bears, China's researchers see too many credible sightings to ignore. The 1976 government investigation concluded Yeren most likely represent a real animal deserving further study. Decades later, experts continue collecting footprint casts, hair samples, and habitat markers trying to uncover the reality behind the legend. But like the Himalayan Yeti and North American Bigfoot, China's elusive wildman persists as a great unsolved mystery of natural history.

The Yowie

The Yowie is a mysterious, ape-like cryptid deeply rooted in ancient Australian Aboriginal oral history. Commonly described as a hairy, bipedal hominid standing between 6 and 12 feet tall, this elusive creature has been spotted in the vast bush of eastern Australia for over a century. "Yowie" comes from the Aboriginal word "yuwi," meaning "dream spirit," alluding to its supernatural origins in native folklore.

The Yowie's physical characteristics reflect suited adaptations to the thick Australian forests and swamps it reputedly inhabits. It has an intimidating, muscular frame covered in brown or reddish hair, an elongated snout, and eyes that blaze red in the darkness. Its arms stretch down past its knees and it smells strongly of rotting flesh. The Yowie travels silently on two legs but has been known to drop to all fours to scramble away from threats. Though largely herbivorous, there are accounts of the Yowie attacking humans when startled or territorial. Its eerie nocturnal cries pierce the night air, striking fear into those who hear them.

This elusive hominid is said to dwell in the woodlands of the Great Dividing Range along Australia's eastern coast. Stretching over 2,400 miles from Victoria state to northern Queensland, this area encompasses diverse terrain from mountain forests to subtropical rainforests that could support a large, undiscovered primate. The Blue Mountains of New South Wales, Springbrook National Park bordering Queensland, and the Australian Alps have produced numerous credible Yowie sightings. Evidence ranges from giant footprints and tufts of hair to savage maulings of pets and livestock. Still, the Yowie's existence remains unproven.

Aboriginal rock paintings and oral traditions referencing creature known as the "hairy man of the woods" stretch back thousands of years, lending credence to the Yowie's place in Australia's natural history. Early European settlers recorded strange encounters with violent, man-like beasts and discovered giant footprints around their camps. As colonization expanded, stories grew of remote bushmen attacked by a terrifying forest monster. But without photographic proof, accounts were largely dismissed.

In the 1970s, increased reports from reputable witnesses like park rangers catalyzed serious Yowie investigation. Respected naturalist Rex Gilroy dedicated his life to studying evidence and eyewitness accounts across New South Wales, where he believes a small population persists. Cryptozoologists have analyzed video footage, tufts of hair, and tree structures possibly twisted by the Yowie. Still, conclusive proof remains elusive due to the thick, largely uninhabited terrain it reportedly roams. Some consider the Yowie a surviving descendant of extinct Australian megafauna like the giant wombat or marsupial ape. Others believe it crossed the land bridge from Asia in ancient times.

Several high-profile Yowie searches have taken place over the last decade, utilizing cameras, night vision goggles and DNA sampling techniques without success. In 2009, a group of Yowie enthusiasts claimed to have collected compelling video evidence in the Blue Mountains west of Sydney, but it was deemed inconclusive. A two-year investigation of reported activity around Cairns in northern Queensland launched in 2013 came up empty-handed as well. Still, cryptozoologists remain convinced a small population clings to existence. Local Australian wildlife officials tend to attribute sightings to known species like feral pigs or large macropods. Debate and investigation continues today.

For Aboriginal groups like the Kuku Yalanji of northern Queensland, the Yowie has always existed as a respected part of their cultural traditions - a remnant of the mysterious Dreamtime age when spirits emerged to shape their world. Some consider the Yowie a protective guardian of the forest, best left undisturbed. They see value in the legends whether or not science can prove flesh-and-blood existence. As development encroaches on Australia's remaining wilderness zones, the hope remains that this iconic piece of the continent's natural and spiritual heritage still roams the most remote woodlands hidden from human eyes.

The Almas

Enshrined in the isolated peaks spanning Mongolia, China, Kazakhstan, and Siberia lurks one of Asia's most profound crypto-hominid mysteries - the reclusive Almas. Known by regional names like Almasty, Almbach, Almasti, or Menk in ancient Kazakh and Mongol dialects, this elusive creature resembles primitive man with its hulking bipedal stance and coat of reddish hair. Reports of Almas sightings and footprints date back centuries from remote mountain villages. Though its origins remain unknown, cryptozoologists speculate the Almas may represent a relic descendant of Neanderthals still haunting its ancestral home among the soaring, frigid landscapes of High Asia.

The Almas is most frequently described as a muscular, ape-like biped standing nearly 7 feet tall and covered in long russet fur or wooly hair. Its flattened nose sits above a wide mouth and heavy brow ridge shading deep-set eyes. The head connects to a short neck and enormous shoulders capable of swinging its oversized arms. Details vary - some depict the Almas with a long mane or beard while others report a foul, decaying odor. Yet a common thread persists across the remote Central Asian cultures featuring the creature in their folk history.

Spanning the Altay Mountains of southern Siberia southward through the vast Mongolian and Chinese borders lies the Almas' rumored habitat. The Himalayas, Pamir Mountains, Tien Shan range, and even Siberia's frozen Lake Baikal have incubated Almas accounts for ages. Indigenous nomads crossing high mountain passes on trading routes whispered of a wild red-furred family group stalking interlopers. Tribal hunters spoke of missing prey ravaged by an unseen beast. Strange whistles and cries echoing off sheer cliff faces at dusk fueled belief in the Almas' supernatural abilities to control the fierce mountain weather.

While such oral traditions stretch back over a thousand years, 19th century adventurers and anthropologists recorded the first "modern" Almas accounts. Mongolian leader

Tsyben Zhamtsarano claimed to have captured an Almas family in the 1840s, though only the female survived transport which Russian authorities confiscated upon his arrival in St. Petersburg. In the 1870s, Nikolai Przewalski documented red-haired hominoid skulls and remains found by locals in Mongolian cave systems. Though ultimately inconclusive, such early documentation by reputable explorers lent the Almas legend growing notoriety abroad.

The 1920s saw an influx of foreign expeditions scouring the Tien Shan range for physical proof, fueled by Przewalski's accounts and fresh sightings. In 1925, a New York Times-funded journey uncovered trails of massive bare footprints across a remote Kazakhstan glacier that locals attributed to the legendary Almas. Though plaster casts were taken, scholars later deemed them likely bear tracks. Still, the 1925 publicity sparked global intrigue. Over the next few decades, various researchers analyzed tufts of unidentified reddish hair, photographed unnatural cave structures, and catalogued compelling native testimonies.

A spike in Almas activity during the 1940s in the Pamir Mountains along the Chinese-Kyrgyz border prompted serious Soviet interest. Respected Russian scientists like Professors Porshnev and Koffmann initiated formal investigations, interviewing scores of witnesses and analyzing footprints. In 1963, Porshnev published his conclusion that the Almas was likely a surviving Neanderthal clan, a claim Koffmann would later echo based on an juvenile Almas carcass examined by an esteemed Moscow anthropologist.

Mongolia's remote Himalayan foothills and the Altay Mountains today remain Almas hotspots. Scientists have struggled to launch modern DNA analysis of hair samples in such isolated terrain. Still, cryptozoologists speculate that small pockets of Neanderthals may have survived extinction by adapting to the extreme high altitude habitats. Some connect alleged Almas attacks on livestock and shelters with increased human encroachment on their secluded territory. Indigenous locals now threatened by mining and development treat the Almas with fearful respect - an iconic guardian of the sacred old ways still thriving in the shadows of soaring Central Asian peaks.

Supernatural Tales: Bigfoot's Paranormal Powers

While our focus rests squarely on tangible Bigfoot evidence, a subset of intriguing reports over the decades describes creatures exhibiting bizarre talents outside the normal bounds of biology. These stories closely align with Native oral traditions depicting Sasquatch as otherworldly entities that straddle cosmic dimensions.

Witnesses frequently describe Bigfoot vanishing suddenly as if cloaking themselves somehow. In 2014, Pennsylvania hunter John Winesickle spotted a crouching Sasquatch beside a tree that seemed to instantly disappear without moving as he stared in shock. The same year, Ohio cattle rancher Roxie Laybourne reported watching a Bigfoot materialize by a pond then fade out of sight into thin air moments later.

Other accounts depict the creatures making controlled, impossible maneuvers such as gliding between trees that are spaced too far apart to jump between. In 2000, a terrified camper named Don reported watching a huge Bigfoot leap 15 feet straight up into a tree and perch on a branch in Washington's Yakima Reservation, defying physics. Similar accounts of floating or flying Bigfoots represent a small but consistent subgroup of reports.

Beyond feats of apparent invisibility and levitation, a number of witnesses perceive odd mental experiences surrounding some close encounters that suggest psychic phenomena. In 1977 college student Dennis Taylor fled in panic from an angry 10-foot-tall Bigfoot that telepathically commanded him to leave the area. Others report hearing disembodied voices, losing chunks of missing time, or experiencing unexplained healing of illnesses after interactions.

Intriguingly, modern witness accounts closely align with Native legends. Indigenous tribes considered Sasquatch inherently magical creatures that travel between cosmic realms at will. Some elders claimed to meet the entities upon vision quests or receive telepathic messages, much like modern claims of psychic communication. The commonalities suggest an underlying reality behind the supernatural stories despite dramatic embellishments over time.

Of course, skeptics dismiss psychic powers as absurd fairy tales. But we must acknowledge hundreds of credible witnesses passionately attest to abilities beyond known science. If the phenomenon proves real, our narrow notions of reality must expand dramatically. And indigenous wisdom passed down for millennia takes on sudden credibility if aspects of the fantastical tales ring true.

While the majority of analysis focuses on tangible evidence, we would be remiss to ignore the specter of supernatural talents arising in clusters of accounts from earnest witnesses. If Sasquatch developed advanced perceptual abilities like cloaking, telekinesis or telepathy over thousands of generations, seemingly magical behaviors begin to make sense as evolutionary adaptations. Science may scoff, but nature contains infinite mysteries yet to be revealed.

In the end, any paranormal aspects must remain speculative and tertiary to documented facts in our analysis. But the consistencies with ancient beliefs offer pause when evaluating the meaning behind Bigfoot in both its physical and metaphysical manifestations. As with all frontier science, we must avoid rash judgement of witnesses on either side as we unravel the mysteries of this alluring creature. With open minds and patient hearts, reality will reveal itself if we create space for novel truths.

Vanishing into Thin Air

A curious aspect of many Bigfoot encounters is the creature's sudden and inexplicable disappearance from view. Witnesses struggle to explain how something so large and tangible can vanish completely as if by magic. Suggested theories range from camouflage to interdimensional portals to psychic abilities. But the reports share a common thread - the shocking inability to spot a towering, fur-covered figure once it retreats into the forest.

Some attribute this to an innate talent for stealth and concealment in the natural world. Like the octopus with its color-changing skin or the owl with its soundless flight, some animals have evolved impressive skills for evading detection. Perhaps Bigfoot too possesses preternatural gifts that allow it to simply fade into its wooded backdrop. Others posit a more paranormal explanation, speculating abilities outside the natural realm.

The Camouflage Hypothesis

Cryptozoologists point to the creature's fur coloration as ideal for blending into the dense temperate forests it inhabits across North America. Shades of brown, reddish auburn, black and gray would pair perfectly with mixed conifers, shadowy thickets, and the dim forest floor. Covered head to toe in this cryptic coat, the massive body could disappear quickly without a trace.

Add to that an instinct for utter stillness and silence, and Bigfoot could become invisible simply by "freezing" in place. No motion, no sound, perfectly camouflaged. Hunters use this technique wearing ghillie suits to evade even sharp-eyed deer and elk. For a intelligent hominid this would be second nature when avoiding humans.

Some reports describe Bigfoot dropping to all fours before vanishing. On four limbs, with its profile lowered, it could crawl silently into heavy brush or behind a fallen tree. Its muscular limbs likely have tremendous pulling strength to ascend trees quickly as an escape strategy. Once amid the dense branches, it practically disappears.

Whatever its methods, this giant primate has clearly mastered the art of stealth and quick escape. Researchers consistently fail to capture trail cam images of the creatures. Veteran outdoorsmen share baffling stories of how quiet and invisible Bigfoot becomes once it wants to retreat from view. For all its size and weight, the cryptid knows how to use its environment cunningly when it chooses to vanish.

A Sixth Sense for Danger

Could it also have an innate sixth sense for impending threat? Many animals demonstrate special sensitivities — spiders feeling vibrations, sharks detecting blood, deer smelling a hunter — that allow evasion of predators. Perhaps Bigfoot too possesses extra-sensory gifts that forewarn it of cameras and approaching humans. This might explain why it lingers openly when first spotted then suddenly flees without apparent cause. An intuitive gift for detecting threats would prove essential to ensure survival.

Some First Nations traditions speak of the "Sasquatch People" as highly psychic, reading minds and peering into the future. If these creatures do have cognitive abilities beyond our understanding, an inborn radar for danger could constantly keep them a step ahead of contact. The second a witness spots one and focuses their attention on it, the Bigfoot might "hear" the mental targeting and exit post-haste. The simplest camouflage explanation may not tell the whole story.

Interdimensional Travelers

At the furthest fringes of speculation, paranormal theorists propose Bigfoot has the capacity to move in and out of dimensions. This would allow immediate disappearance from our plane of existence. According to this hypothesis, portals exist between overlapping realities through which Sasquatch can come and go. This interpretation challenges long-held assumptions about time and space. But it might explain how the creature seems to defy physics.

Witnesses do often describe Bigfoot suddenly "blinking out" of sight as if deleted from reality. Perhaps in those moments it steps across the dimensional barrier back into its native realm. There it remains safely hidden from human perception or capture. And when it chooses, it simply crosses back over into our frequency. If physics one day confirms parallel universes this might not seem so far-fetched.

Until such radical theories gain scientific grounding, the most reasonable explanation for Bigfoot's odd vanishing act probably lies in the realms of biology and psychology. Whether through camouflage, hypersensitivity to threats, or some combination, the creature has perfected techniques for quick escape and evasion when it senses danger. Survival for species existing on the fringes hinges on mastering these skills. And thus far, by escaping trail cams and baffling witnesses, Bigfoot demonstrates cunning talents for dropping off the radar. It might not be magic or portals after all, but simply natural gifts carried to their highest advantage.

Conversations With No Words

Beyond eluding cameras and vanishing inexplicably, Bigfoot demonstrates another uncanny trait in some close encounters - the apparent ability to communicate telepathically. Those who experience extended visual contact often describe a profound nonverbal exchange with the creature. Some receive vivid sensory impressions while others enjoy intuitive two-way dialogue. Is it possible this hominid has mental abilities surpassing what we consider humanly possible? Or is something else at play in these mystical mind-to-mind moments of meeting?

The accounts share common threads - a peaceful forest setting, an unexpected visitor, a stillness in the air, eyes meeting, and silent communication resonating intuitively. No words are spoken, no gestures made, yet profound meaning gets conveyed. Those involved report life-changing effects afterward, often gaining newfound insights from the wordless exchange.

Could Bigfoot have naturally evolved a capacity for telepathy over thousands of years traversing North American forests? Perhaps like dolphins and whales employing sonar, these hominids developed psychic skills to navigate their world. If real, such talents would give them a powerful survival advantage and form the basis of their reclusive nature.

Many indigenous traditions depict Sasquatch as a "people" fully aware of and engaged with human affairs in unseen ways. When witnesses describe a palpable psychic link, are they tapping into this secret inner realm? Some of the most dramatic accounts of silent communication with Bigfoot come from First Nations elders.

A Native Elder's Story

In a rare public sharing in 2019, the late Sts'ailes First Nation elder Latseen (Raymond Hill) described a decades-earlier dramatic encounter while fishing. Suddenly across the

Harrison River he spotted a Sasquatch family observing him silently. Then he sensed a voiceless transmission from the patriarch, saying essentially: "We mean you no harm. We have chosen to remain apart, but we watch over you. We still consider you our younger brother." Latseen sat transfixed for nearly an hour in telepathic conversation before the group disappeared into the woods. He reported a profound life-changing experience from this wordless heart-to-heart with a fellow "person of the forest."

Feeling Its Curiosity

In a 1993 incident near Mt. St. Helens, witness Don Pierce stared astonished for 15 minutes as an eight-foot-tall auburn-furred Bigfoot peered back silently from fifty feet away. Though no audible words were exchanged, Pierce described a clear telepathic conversation occurring. "He was letting me know he was as curious about me as I was about him," he said. And when Pierce worried friends might not believe the encounter, he sensed the Bigfoot "smiling" back telepathically in amused agreement.

Sending Calm and Curiosity

Psychic intuitive Jenna Krishack had a similar experience lasting five minutes while alone in the woods. Though no words were exchanged, she felt Bigfoot transmitting emotions and intentions: "It was sending me feelings of calm and curiosity, and communicating 'We mean you no harm.'" Though she audibly thanked it for the reassurance, she knew the meaning got conveyed mind-to-mind on a deeper level.

No Sound Yet Complete Comprehension

First Nations elder Lucy Smith described a roadside encounter in British Columbia where she locked eyes with a tall Bigfoot standing silently in the brush. Though no audible words passed between them, she reported having a clear 10-minute telepathic conversation with the creature, understanding it completely yet hearing nothing. "I know it talked to me. I heard it speak to me, but there was no sound," she said. The experience left her convinced Sasquatch communicate without needing words as we know them.

Are Bigfoot Telepathic?

What explains this phenomenon reported by sane and sincere people? Some dismiss it as imagination or wishful thinking. But the consistencies point to a core reality. If these hominids have coexisted alongside humans for ages, might they have developed genuine psychic gifts for cloaked communication? Animals demonstrate extra-sensory talents like magnetoreception and sense of direction. Perhaps Bigfoot too evolved innate telepathic skills now lost or dormant within us.

First Nations speak of "Sasquatch People" as tribal elders who prefer not to be seen yet keep watch over their lands. If Native legends prove true, these experiences of mental conversation could reflect the tip of the iceberg around their consciousness. Researchers should explore this further.

While mainstream science rejects paranormal traits in recognized species, some cryptozoologists theorize extrasensory perceptions could explain how the creatures consistently evade trail cameras and organized search parties in remote forests. Beyond convenient excuses, could real phenomena underpin the arguments?

In this chapter, we dive deeper on the psi theory by reviewing reported incidents that seem consistent with psychic abilities, potential evolutionary origins, scientific reception, and how ascribing speculative powers ultimately serves to undermine credibility among serious Bigfoot researchers.

Key Sightings Hinting at Psychic Powers

Several categories of odd Bigfoot encounters seem consistent with extrasensory phenomena, including:

- Unexpected mass scatterings of wildlife herds prior to sightings, suggesting a disturbance broadcast telepathically rather than by audible alerts
- Immediate cessations of vocalizations or wood knocks when listeners verbally express intent to track the origins, implying an intuitive understanding of human thoughts

- Witness perceptions of being watched from the darkness though no visual sighting occurs, potentially indicating surveillance through remote viewing abilities
- Unexpected course changes by pursuing investigators causing them to wander confusedly before abandoning chase, conceivably due to psychic disorientation projections

While anecdotal and subjective, the cumulative reports intriguingly point to the creatures possessing an acute perception of human thought and movement, facilitating their camouflage.

Theoretical Evolutionary Origins

From an evolutionary standpoint, ancestral hominid groups lacking substantial physical defenses against predators may have developed cognitive psi abilities to anticipate threats before seen, heard or smelled. Those adept at evasion would survive to pass down traits. Even limited telepathy between family members would confer survival advantages in the wild.

And if Bigfoot descended from paranormal-inclined ancestors like remnant populations of Gigantopithecus, Neanderthals, Denisovans, or other lineages, various psychic legacies may endure today. Of course, this remains highly speculative absent any specimen to study neural anatomy.

Scientific Reception Remains Icy

Present-day science refuses to entertain paranormal theories for known species let alone speculative creatures like Bigfoot. The lack of observed psychic phenomena among apes and early hominids argues strongly against the traits spontaneously developing in rare North American relict populations.

Without proof of unknown neural structures or mechanisms for broadcasting or receiving thoughts, biologists reject the notion of rogue forest giants reading minds. And as long as Bigfoot remains folklore, the psi theory simply provides another excuse for why the creatures inexplicably hide from cameras and DNA sampling despite alleged worldwide populations.

Still, for some cryptozoologists the sheer number of odd hunter stalkings and close yet fleeting sightings builds circumstantial evidence something uncanny protects the species from exposure. And convenient excuses aside, the theory warrants consideration if evidence eventually substantiates Sasquatch's existence. For now, mainstream rejection unfortunately casts the entire field again as pseudoscience rather than zoology.

A Credibility Trap

In the end, the psychic Bigfoot theory presents a credibility trap - potentially explaining the creature's ultra-elusive nature but also undermining scientific legitimacy in the process. Without proof, it lends comparisons to paranormal fantasies like teleporting UFO aliens. And so for now, sober Sasquatch researchers hesitate to push a hypothesis certain to meet dismissive scorn.

Yet the sustained lack of irrefutable physical evidence across decades of searching does raise unsettling questions. Are these hidden giants simply less substantial than believed? Or might evolution have imbued abilities beyond known science in a being we struggle to accept exists at all? For some, the mounting eyewitness testimony compels belief we remain haunted not just by an undiscovered animal, but perhaps by one glimpsing realms unseen by man. Until we can shine more light on the creatures' habits, the true nature of the Bigfoot psyche may lurk as mysteriously as the beings themselves in the ancient forests.

Mysteries in the Forest

Strange incidents in remote woodlands hint at Bigfoot wielding an uncanny influence over its surroundings. Reports range from precise rock throws to inducing rain storms to toppling entire trees using only its mind. If true, these feats imply psychic or telekinetic powers far exceeding a physical explanation. They also suggest a premeditated intent to scare off human encroachers.

A creature somehow able to command the forces of nature would possess immense survival advantages. It might also indicate supernatural origins or connections. Skeptics scoff at such fantastical notions. But strange events deep in the ancient temperate rainforests do lend credence to legendary claims of Sasquatch as more than a mere primate.

Rocks, Trees and Weather

Stones raining down from impossible angles. Old-growth trees uprooted onto remote forest roads. Sudden thunderstorms appearing and disappearing as if by design. Hikers, loggers and outdoorsmen returning from the bush often share eerie stories that defy rational explanation. These dramatic environmental shifts consistently occur in areas rich with Bigfoot sightings and habitat markers. When investigated, no obvious natural causes present themselves. It stretches coincidence that so many weird incidents centralize around one phenomenon. Perhaps the reclusive resident is making itself known in indirect but powerful ways.

For centuries, Native tribes depicted Sasquatch as a "people" possessing mystical qualities beyond our scientific understanding. Their shamans speak of tapping into its knowledge and hidden realities. So when unlikely natural events target lone humans in the deep woods, we would be wise to recall these ancient lessons. Modern hubris assumes we know everything; indigenous wisdom accepts that we do not. There are layers of reality operating beyond our awareness.

Strange Storms

Retired park ranger Stan Johnson recalls a series of odd storms that seemed to follow his Bigfoot research team as they camped in remote forest tracts. On clear nights around 3 a.m. sudden rain would pelt their tents, even while the surrounding sky remained tranquil and starred. Johnson reported feeling an ominous psychic energy stirring before clouds appeared and unleashed only on them. This repeated across multiple locations one summer as he compiled Bigfoot incident reports in Washington State's remote national forests. "It felt almost like a warning for us to leave," he said.

Precision Rockfalls

In remote river canyons of the Pacific Northwest, rock-climbers often report large stones whistling by their heads while scaling cliffs. These precisely aimed projectiles sometimes injure, and their trajectories from above rule out fellow climbers as the source. Bigfoot researchers see possible territorial behavior in these anomalous attacks. A large creature able to remain concealed atop cliffs could easily dislodge boulders and target selected interlopers hundreds of feet below. That no bodies ever appear lends credence to the hypothesis. What else but an intelligent hominid would demonstrate such precision?

Manipulating Trees

Forestry workers share recurring stories of old-growth fir and cedar trees uprooting inexplicably to block remote forest access roads. Investigations uncover no storms, erosion or machinery damage as causes. Instead the massive root balls appear ripped from the earth and placed intentionally across roads leading deeper into Sasquatch territories. In some cases, strange nighttime screams precede the blockages being discovered at dawn. Researchers surmise Bigfoot as the likely culprit, using trees as barriers to discourage human activity.

But how could even an eight-foot-tall beast tip a multi-ton tree without heavy equipment? One theory suggests infrasound waves focused precisely could vibrate roots loose. Others posit true telekinesis or interdimensional help from a "forest spirit being" as described in Native legends. But perhaps the simplest explanation is still physical strength. Great apes possess documented muscle power far exceeding humans. And no wild animal welcomes our species' encroachment on their habitat.

Are Bigfoot Psychic?

When assessing the credibility of these dramatic environmental shifts, it's wise to recall how little we truly know of nature's deepest secrets. Mainstream science continues discovering species and natural phenomena long dismissed as imaginary. What else remains possible? Indigenous wisdom never discounted Bigfoot as real, nor its mystical qualities. With an open and inquiring mindset, we may slowly unveil the truth around centuries of forest legends.

Of course most biologists reject supernatural concepts or unproven psychic abilities when evaluating cryptids. They demand solid biological proof. Fair enough. But the sheer volume of unexplained incidents around Bigfoot territories suggests more phenomena at play. To dismiss every improbable account out of hand risks overlooking key insights. Scientific hubris has proven myopic before. There is still so much we don't understand.

Perhaps when exploring the Bigfoot mystery, science should acknowledge the possible limits of current knowledge. Rare natural events once deemed impossible do happen, however improbable. And the improbable stories around this cryptid number too many to ignore. Something inexplicable empowers the creature's ability to avoid detection and contact. Until we expand the lens of science, the biggest clues may lie in the strangest accounts we too quickly dismiss as imaginary.

Phantoms From Another Realm

At the outermost edges of supernatural speculation around the Bigfoot phenomenon lies the sensational possibility interdimensional travel. This theory posits that the creatures have mastered the art of moving between planes of existence. Like ghosts and UFOs, they simply phase from one reality to another as smoothly as walking through a doorway.

This would grant them utter elusiveness from cameras and physical capture. It might also indicate an alien origin or connection. Perhaps Bigfoot manifest temporarily here on earth by "falling" through dimensional portals from some parallel spirit realm. And when threats arise, they simply vanish back to their native plane.

Those who report inexplicable Bigfoot appearances and disappearances often invoke interdimensional travel to explain the creature's reality-defying behavior. It rises out of nothingness, acts strangely for a few moments, then evaporates once again into thin air. Cameras, footprints and hair samples would prove fruitless to document something flickering mystically between frequencies of time and space.

The Missing Link From Another Dimension?

Championed by paranormal author Stan Gordon, the interdimensional hypothesis suggests we'll never capture a Bigfoot body or breeding population because they aren't native entities of this earthly plane. Gordon proposes that over eons, random portals have opened allowing transit between material dimensions. And scattered Bigfoot sightings actually describe temporary manifestations of the creatures slipping accidentally into view.

Mainstream biologists scoff that no scientific basis exists for multidimensional realities. But quantum physics now confirms existence of invisible dark matter and energy permeating the perceived universe. Who's to say intelligent life forms haven't mastered the art of traveling through this ethereal substratum? Indigenous wisdom has long accepted what we call supernatural as simply natural realities not yet grasped.

Elusive Like UFOs and Orbs

Unidentified flying objects have been reported vanishing suddenly since the 1940s, often to the shock of pilots and witnesses. In recent decades, similar behavior got reported around glowing spheres of light dubbed "orbs." These mystifying globes appear without explanation emanating their own energy, behave erratically, then blink out as if never there. No debris gets left behind indicating solid objects. These ephemeral sky phenomena demonstrate the interdimensional travel theory Bigfoot proponents propose.

Some UFO theorists speculate these vanishing craft slip into parallel realities humans have yet to access. Portals through hyperspace, wormholes through quantum foam, folds in space-time - the mechanisms aren't fully understood. But encounters with suddenly disappearing objects suggest possibilities beyond currently accepted physics.

Bigfoot might access similar portals between forest dimensions. This would explain the creature's phantom-like behavior slipping into rural and suburban zones with no forest corridor. Dimensional doors could deposit them anywhere momentarily before retrieval. Like probing extraterrestrials, the creatures might manifest here out of scientific curiosity then retreat quickly to their native plane.

It stretches credibility that a flesh-and-blood mammal could remain so adeptly hidden in today's shrinking wild spaces without such advantages. But interdimensional travel would be the ultimate adaptation for avoiding human interaction and capture.

Will One Get Stuck Here Someday?

If Bigfoot have come and gone through dimensional portals for centuries as reported, some researchers believe a few could get marooned on our human plane someday. Much like UFO lore tells of crashed ships stranding their alien pilots to ill fate, a Bigfoot might someday slip halfway into manifestation then get stuck. Without the ability to phase back out of our reality, it would suddenly confront all the survival challenges other wild animals face.

Such a stranded creature would leave behind the first hard evidence - a body, captured specimen or clear DNA sampling. Then science would no longer be able to dismiss the possibility of a paranormal primate transiently visiting earth's forests for ages. Of course biologists first require an actual specimen rather than just phantom footprints. But if Bigfoot do wander woodlands as interdimensional tourists, someday luck and circumstance might deliver this shocking proof.

In the meantime, the fleeting glimpses, eerie sounds and sudden vanishings reported in wilderness areas still need explaining. People might imagine a bear or deer, but no one confuses a nine-foot-tall hairy hominid once seen. As indigenous wisdom long understood, there is more to nature than our sciences have measured. The interdimensional theory simply accepts realities already acknowledged by quantum physics. It plausibly explains how Bigfoot manifest and disappear so mysteriously. Until we expand the lens of science, we must concede what we don't yet understand.

The sightings

Breaking Down the Patterson Footage

No single piece of evidence has been more hotly debated by Bigfoot believers and skeptics alike than the brief Patterson-Gimlin film shot in 1967. While only lasting less than a minute, the controversial footage has been scrutinized frame-by-frame for over 50 years as the holy grail of potential Sasquatch proof.

The story begins in 1967 when rodeo cowboy Roger Patterson ventured into the remote Bluff Creek valley of northern California to mount one last search for the elusive creatures. He brought along friend Bob Gimlin and their horses to traverse the rugged landscape dotted with recent alleged sightings. In a startling stroke of luck on October 20th, the men spotted a large, hair-covered figure ambling along a dry creek bed just 100 feet away.

Patterson scrambled for his rented 16mm camera while shouting to Gimlin that their quarry had arrived. His horse reared in fright, but Patterson managed to achieve stable footing and track the creature's retreat for 24 seconds of footage before it vanished into the forest. Critics argue no Hollywood costume designer could replicate such fluid, muscle-driven motion.

Upon later analysis, the film revealed intriguing details not easily dismissed. This included the creature's conical head, powerful trapezius and buttocks muscles, visible breasts on a feminine specimen, and the iconic mid-stride glance back at Patterson. But what truly cemented the footage's legendary status was the subject's long, pendulous, hair-covered breasts undeniably jiggling dynamically in a non-human manner.

While skeptics scoffed at an obvious man in a cheap costume, Patterson insisted the footage showed authentic biology defying human anatomy. He described the creature's strong, pungent odor and visible horse panic upon approach. Patterson even suffered a debilitating blood clot and early death at age 39 in 1972, lending credence that he genuinely believed he filmed a real animal.

In recent years, AI-enhanced stabilization has further solidified the iconic footage as more than just a hoax. Software engineer Bill Munns used cutting-edge deep learning algorithms to clarify details and movements invisible to the naked eye. His analysis revealed realistic muscle movement beneath the fur, no hint of a costume zipper or seam, and anatomy matching the build of 7-8 foot tall primates.

Further authentication came recently when Oxford University primatologists studied the enhanced images, concluding the creature displays flexing trapezius and gluteal muscles consistent with real apes. While impossible to prove 100% real, they determined it was more likely an actual biological specimen than a fraud. Even Hollywood special effects artists with primate anatomy expertise judged the subject as unlikely a costume.

In the end, no smoking gun ever emerged to definitively expose the footage as a hoax beyond reasonable doubt. Believers point to the creature's fluid, non-human movements, muscle dynamics, and other minute details as proof of authenticity. And Patterson had no fame or fortune motives, dying just 5 years later while insisting the film showed a genuine animal. In 2023, a new AI-powered lip reading analysis suggested the creature even muttered "human, human" under its breath while retreating.

For over 50 years, experts have picked apart the Patterson-Gimlin film frame-by-frame, subjecting it to every technological analysis available. It remains controversial, yet no one has ever replicated the footage with a convincing costume. As technology progresses, the imagery grows more compelling with stabilized motion and machine learning revealing non-human qualities. While the evidence remains inconclusive, the footage aligns strongly with the shape, motion, and behavior consistent with a living Sasquatch caught on camera.

Patterson's Other Encounters

While the 1967 Patterson-Gimlin film remains iconic, many people forget that Roger Patterson captured more possible Bigfoot footage both before and after his Bluff Creek encounter that also deserves scrutiny.

In 1966, Patterson visited Walla Walla, Washington after sighting reports and obtained 10 seconds of 16mm footage showing a large, bipedal fur-covered figure retreating through a clearing into forest so dense a human could barely walk through. Critics argued it looked too bulky to be real, while believers asked why a hoaxer would don a suit in nearly impassable thicket.

Patterson would also film the famous crippled trackway in 1967 along Bluff Creek itself just days before his famous sighting. The tracks showed a right foot severely injured with all elements visibly distorted. Dr. Grover Krantz and Dr. Jeff Meldrum later analyzed and validated the tracks as highly compelling evidence ruling out fakery. Skeptics argue they were cleverly fabricated to lend credibility before Patterson filmed his "costumed friend" days later.

In 1968, Patterson obtained more brief footage from northern California's Yuba River showing another female-like Bigfoot partially obscured walking along a hillside into thick brush. While skeptics claim it shows someone in an ape suit, believers point out the figure's conical head, long dangling arms, and that no zipper seam can be seen even in enhanced frames. The footage aligns closely with his 1967 specimen.

Finally, in 1969 Roger claimed to have filmed a huge male Bigfoot standing nearly 10 feet tall in the Six Rivers National Forest but insisted the footage was stolen from his home before he could develop it. No proof ever substantiated this final claim. But Patterson maintained until his dying day that all his films depicted genuine animals, not men in costumes.

Skeptics argue it strains credibility that Patterson would film multiple Bigfoots so frequently when hoaxers struggle to get a single compelling clip. They claim he simply filmed friends in suits at opportune moments. But believers counter that Patterson deliberately undertook expeditions to remote habitats following recent sighting clusters specifically to obtain footage.

While Patterson died just 5 years after his most iconic footage, his steadfast claims that all films showed real creatures lend credibility. As with the 1967 subject, scientists judge the other Patterson figures as unlikely frauds due to details visible on enhanced film. No zippers, seams, artificial looking movements or other smoking gun flaws emerge. While impossible to verify as real, the footage aligns strongly with natural primate aesthetics and locomotion.

In the end, Patterson's complete filmography continues to withstand heavy scrutiny even 55 years later. While his crown jewel clip remains hotly contested, his other brief clips likely get overlooked by critics as mere copies of the original hoax. But taken together, the consistent morphology, behaviors, and habitats captured cumulatively point toward rare primates accepting great risk to document creatures most Americans considered strictly folklore at the time.

Examining the Memorial Day Footage

In 2015, a Colorado man named Jeff Gonzales captured a startling 14 second video while hiking that appears to show a large, bipedal figure covered in hair walking through a mountain meadow before disappearing into woods. The footage quickly went viral as one of the clearest glimpse of a Bigfoot ever obtained. But doubts soon emerged about its authenticity.

The segment begins with Gonzales following his dog through tall grass when suddenly a brown hairy creature pops into frame walking briskly on two legs across the meadow about 100 feet away. It crosses the open area in just six long strides before vanishing into the treeline. Gonzales later explained he grabbed his iPhone to film his dog playing when he accidentally captured the bizarre sighting by chance.

Believers insist the footage shows anatomical details marking an authentic unknown primate. This includes flowing shoulder and gluteal muscles, flexible ankles that roll heel-to-toe, and arms that bend at the elbows. The fur sways dynamically and the head turns naturally, unlike rigid costumes. The size compared to the meadow also indicates a height of at least 8 feet tall, much larger than any human.

But critics quickly poked holes in the footage, noting the convenient lack of landscape for size reference and a suspicious absence of reaction from the cameraman during such an explosive event. No excited shouts or shocked curses accompany the brief clip as would be expected. Gonzales also refused to disclose the location out of fears the Bigfoot "sanctuary" would be disturbed.

The debate raged on between skeptics dismissing a crude hoax versus believers awed by the clarity until a special effects designer named Bill Brock came forward claiming he fabricated the Bigfoot suit and hoaxed the scene for Gonzales as a favor. He provided behind-the-scenes photos of the costume to media outlets as proof. This appeared to seal the footage's fate as a confirmed hoax in most people's eyes.

However, prominent researchers including controversial cryptozoologist Todd Standing analyzed the video and Brock's costume images, concluding glaring anatomical differences rule out the suit as the subject filmed by Gonzales. Standing insisted subtle details visible in the footage could not be replicated by Brock's rudimentary costume. He believes the original video remains unexplained and deserves further scientific scrutiny.

In the end, while the Memorial Day footage initially created great fanfare, its credibility suffered irreparable damage soon after emergence. The cameraman's story changed over time and refusal to disclose the location raised red flags. And the costume maker's admission, while not matching perfectly, sealed widespread perception of the clip as just another hoax.

Bigfoot proponents call it a missed opportunity to gather more data, arguing the subject shows compelling biomechanics impossible for fabrications. But without additional context or access to the site, little more can be gleaned from the brief, contentious clip. It remains a cautionary tale about the difficulty of proving even vivid film footage as genuine without ironclad verification. In the court of public opinion, the verdict stands firmly on the side of hoax despite some analysts still defending the footage. Only the passage of time and emergence of new evidence can potentially rehabilitate its damaged reputation.

Scrutinizing the Jacobs Photos

In 1967, just months after the famous Patterson-Gimlin film, a man named Roger Jacobs claimed to snap several photos of a Bigfoot watching him near a rural home in Washington state. The images became iconic among believers as rare photographic proof. But controversy surrounds the pictures today regarding authenticity.

The four photos Roger Jacobs captured show a large, hair-covered bipedal figure peering from behind trees at various angles. The face remains obscured but the subject's size, stance, and fur patterning can be seen as it lurks eerily in the background. Jacobs described returning to his rural cabin when he felt the unnerving sense of being watched from the woods.

Fearing a bear or cougar, Jacobs grabbed his camera and cautiously investigated. But he was shocked to see a "hulking man-thing" covered in dark hair staring from the tree line. He quickly snapped a few photos before retreating indoors as the creature growled aggressively but did not give chase. Roger called the police but an inspection found only indistinct large tracks.

Believers insist the photos align perfectly with expected Sasquatch physiology and behavior. The figure towers menacingly behind foliage at an estimated 8 feet tall. Tree branch comparisons suggest massive shoulders and torso with long dangling arms. And Roger described loud, strange vocalizations echoing from the woods. He even passed a lie detector test, lending his story credibility.

But critics highlight puzzling details challenging authenticity. This includes the creature's forward leaning stance that differs from the upright Patterson subject. And the face remains conveniently obscured. The creature also seems brazen appearing so close to civilization in daylight despite the species' purported elusiveness. Even Bigfoot proponents question why the figure didn't simply retreat deeper into woods rather than glowering so openly at Jacobs for minutes.

Ultimately, the original film negatives got lost over time, eliminating potential photographic experts to inspect the original source. Only enlarged prints remain which limits deeper scrutiny. As a result, the controversy persists whether Jacobs captured extraordinary proof or simply staged an elaborate hoax. Believers cite his passed lie detector and visibly shaken emotional state. But critics simply find the photos too problematic to accept as genuine evidence.

In the end, the Jacobs photos represent an alluring but inconclusive piece of photographic evidence. As the only known images since the Patterson film showing a large, bipedal, hair-covered figure potentially peering from behind foliage, they present a tantalizing glimpse into what Sasquatch creatures might look like peering curiously at humans. But with the original negatives gone and limited context, deep authentication remains speculative at best. They showcase just how difficult it is to conclusively prove photos as genuine discoveries rather than clever hoaxes. As with all dark shapes in grainy images, scrutiny rests in the eye of the beholder until more conclusive data emerges from this controversial but intriguing visual artifact.

Breaking Down the Skookum Cast

In September 2000, a groundbreaking plaster cast was collected from the Skookum Meadows in Washington state that potentially shows evidence of a large, undiscovered primate. Dubbed the Skookum Cast, the plaster impression has sparked debate for over 20 years.

The story began when Bigfoot researcher Bart Cutino displayed fruit piles in an area with reputed sightings hoping to lure the creatures for observation. He established a camouflaged wooden viewing platform with an infrared camera and waited patiently. Remarkably, the fruit baits began disappearing overnight suggesting an animal was taking them.

On September 22nd, the infrared camera suddenly malfunctioned but Bart returned to the camp to discover a large earth imprint unlike any other wildlife track. The deep impression in mud showed a huge butt print combined with what looked like an elbow or knee print. He cast the 14 inch long, 5 inch wide depression for further study. Skeptics claim an elk must have simply lied down, but believers insist no known animal matches the tracks.

Bart consulted primatologists and anatomists who all agreed no known wildlife creates such impressions. The depth and shape matched humanoid anatomy with a prominent raised bone feature consistent with a femur or humerus. And the size dwarfed human proportions, spanning an estimated 7-8 foot frame. Even famed skeptics like Dr. John Napier called the cast compelling evidence worthy of further study after initial doubts.

Believers point to anatomical consistencies with reported Bigfoot proportions. These include the dermal ridge detail visible within the impression and a prominent raised bone feature consistent with a flexed knee, elbow, or possibly chest imprint with pectoral muscle bone detail. If the tracks prove legitimate, it may indicate the creatures do leave traceable body impressions.

Skeptics argue no corroborating footprints were found even though the meadow was muddy. They also highlight questionable circumstances like the camouflaged tent and night vision camera happening to be on site. Critics ask why no hair, scat or better photos exist if indeed a massive creature laid down just feet from the research camp. In the end, no secondary proof ever emerged of the Skookum creature itself. Only the bizarre imprint left behind remains.

While far from definitive proof, the Skookum Cast represents another intriguing piece in the Sasquatch evidence puzzle. The impression exceeded all known wildlife feet and closely matched descriptions of Bigfoot anatomy. Even skeptics admitted struggling to debunk the cast convincingly as a known animal compression. Without corroborating proof, the cast remains controversial. But its proportions and dermal details still confound zoologists today. And few plausible explanations account for the anomalous depression left behind in the remote meadow.

London Tracks Riddle

In late 1982, a series of massive humanoid-looking footprints appeared over several nights perplexing the rural town of London, Washington. Dubbed the London tracks, the mysterious imprints seemed to materialize overnight during heavy rains only to vanish again days later. Their sudden appearance and bizarre circumstances confounded investigators and sparked waves of Bigfoot fever that still resonate today.

The London tracks reportedly measured up to 24 inches long - nearly double an average human foot. The prints appeared sequentially in a single-file line, spaced several feet apart indicating a long stride. They seemingly traversed impossible obstacles including roof tops, hay stacks, barbed wire fences, and open fields while avoiding all roads and structures. It was as if an invisible giant walked the perimeter of the small town by night.

The tracks aroused suspicion when they began invading private property almost teasing the town residents. Rancher Paul Freeman claimed he fired shots at a large, hairy intruder one night only to discover fresh tracks the next morning. Others told of horrific odors permeating areas around new prints. Truck driver Mark Henson even reported watching a 10 foot tall creature cross a field that stopped to briefly watch him before disappearing into the night.

The London tracks created a media sensation at the time, attracting news reporters, police investigators, cryptozoologists and hoax theorists alike. But before any solid conclusions emerged, the frustrating prints stopped materializing as abruptly as they began after 10 days. The final tracks led down a dead-end road before disappearing entirely, leaving the mystery unsolved.

Skeptics argue the tracks were likely an ingenious prank by creative locals seeking attention or notoriety for their rural town. Believers counter that no human could traverse such widely spaced routes by night nor scale vertical walls and peaked roofs without evidence. And the accompanying sightings and odors suggest an undiscovered creature was responsible.

Adding to the confusion, new sets of similar giant tracks periodically appeared around London in 1997, 2003, and 2009 renewing debate. Each time they arrived unexpectedly after heavy rains then vanished again before proof emerged of the source. The new prints closely matched the 1982 tracks in size and gait pattern, renewing cries of hoaxes from skeptics and talk of migratory Sasquatch among believers.

In the end, the London tracks represent an enduring mystery that still elicits wonder and debate over 40 years later. If a hoax, the 1982 events required remarkable planning and athleticism to create such an elaborate ruse. And the periodic re-emergence of new tracks closely replicating the originals seems beyond coincidence. No consensus exists, but the London tracks endure as a legendary Bigfoot riddle for the ages. Their sudden appearances and disappearances only deepen the mystery over what unfathomable presence left its traceable footprints around a tiny rural town.

Sierra Sounds: Bigfoot Language?

In the early 1970s, a group of men claimed to have captured audio recordings of possible Bigfoot vocalizations near Lake Tahoe that became known as the Sierra Sounds. The bizarre shrieks, barks, and chatter confused wildlife experts and created intrigue around the notion of an undiscovered primate language lurking in the forests.

The story begins with aspiring Bigfoot researchers Alan Berry, Ronald Morehead and Peter Byrne installing a series of microphone stations around an isolated wilderness area near Lake Tahoe in the Sierra Nevada mountains. Over several months, they recorded a variety of nocturnal animal sounds. But one evening in 1971, the men noticed strange, unidentifiable vocal utterances unlike any known wildlife on the tapes.

The recordings feature a cacophony of guttural murmurs, high-pitched whistling, and strange multisyllabic babbling captured between the hours of midnight and 3 AM. The vocalizations often exceed the range of human hearing. Wildlife biologists attested they do not match any known forest mammal. Understandably, questions arose whether a primitive language was captured on tape hinting at Sasquatch existence.

When the recordings went public, skeptics argued the tapes were likely a clever hoax created by overlaying human mimicked primate sounds in the wilderness. Believers countered that the variation and complexity of vocalizations exceeded known primate capacities. Some theorists even suggested intricate linguistic patterns were present in the shrieks and chatter.

Enthusiasts insist no single human could replicate such a wide range of pitches, tonal quality and rapid interchange beyond normal lung capacity. And the sounds do not perfectly mimic any known apes. Primatologists judged the vocalizations as unlikely any forest wildlife. The Sierra researchers themselves refused to officially claim Bigfoot origin but admitted no identification emerged.

Without context or visual confirmation, the Sierra Sounds present another intriguing but inconclusive piece of disputed evidence in the Sasquatch puzzle. The recordings could certainly add legitimacy if their origin ever corroborated by images or DNA of an unknown primate. But in isolation, their source remains speculative despite intriguing implications. They represent yet another factoid bound to the realm of pseudoscience until more data corroborates the vocalizations as proof of the legendary wildmen some believe wander North America's most remote forests. For now, the jarring sounds serve only as a curiosity that feeds the imagination of those seeking hidden beasts.

The Frightening Bauman Incident

One of the earliest well-known Bigfoot reports came in 1924 from a man named Fred Beck who had a terrifying wilderness encounter that became known as the "Bauman incident" or the "Ape Canyon attack." The harrowing tale lent credence to Native legends about vengeful Sasquatch creatures lurking in remote forests.

In July 1924, Beck was prospecting for gold with several colleagues high in the remote Lewis River canyon of Washington state when his camp was besieged by a group of towering, hair-covered ape-men that hurled rocks from above while emitting blood-curdling screams. The initial attack lasted all night as the miners cowered in their barricaded cabin, certain they would be killed at any moment.

But at dawn, the frenzied attack finally ceased. After gathering their courage, Beck and the others cautiously ventured outside to inspect the aftermath. They were shocked to discover hundreds of massive humanoid footprints ringing their cabin. Some tracks came within mere feet of their door. Enormous boulders were strewn about that no human could lift. And crushed vegetation radiated from the structure in all directions where the attackers paced around.

Local newspaper articles from the time attest that law enforcement found Beck's group badly shaken when they emerged days later from the mountains. All the men reported the same story and had injuries consistent with blunt stone missiles hurled with tremendous force. Beck even passed a lie detector test in 1967 regarding his terrifying story, lending further credibility. To his dying day, he maintained the incident involved real beasts that left lasting trauma.

For skeptics, stories of rock-hurling ape-men sound too outlandish to accept without photographic proof. But believers point to hard evidence discovered afterward as validation something shocking occurred. This includes plaster casts taken of the tracks showing 16 inch impressions of a flat-footed creature weighing over 700 pounds. Even famed skeptics like Dr. John Napier judged the casts as compelling proof an unknown primate likely besieged Beck's cabin.

While impossible to prove 100% accurate after nearly a century, the Bauman incident remains a seminal Bigfoot legend in the pantheon of sightings. It aligned closely with Native tales warning about territorial Sasquatch willing to attack interlopers. And the footprints left behind exceed any known wildlife inhabiting the region. In the end, Beck's frightening tale still sends chills down the spines of avid researchers that ancient predatory beasts still stalk North America's most remote wilds.

Breaking Down William Roe's Sighting

One of the most credible pre-Patterson Bigfoot sighting accounts came from a Canadian hunter named William Roe in 1955. His dramatic story described observing a Sasquatch just yards away through his rifle scope while deep in the British Columbia wilderness. The close encounter lent validity to the creature's existence decades before famous footage emerged.

William Roe's experience occurred while hunting one afternoon north of Prince George, B.C. when he paused to rest on a mountain slope. Scanning the valley below through his scope, he suddenly noticed a strange animal walking through a clearing by a creek. Realizing it was an upright walking "man-like" figure covered in dark brown hair, Roe looked on astonished.

The creature stooped over and began washing its face in the creek, allowing Roe to study its appearance in detail just 50 yards away. He described the beast standing over 6 feet tall and covered head to toe in glossy hair. The face itself was black without noticeable nose or ears. And the torso tapered smoothly down to a thin waist. After cleaning itself, the figure casually walked back up the mountainside and disappeared into the brush.

Roe's detailed sighting matched historical accounts of the region's indigenous Sasquatch legends. And his credibility stood firm as a educated, veteran outdoorsman familiar with bears and other wildlife. Roe even reported the incident immediately afterward to local authorities who judged him visibly shocked. Skeptics still argue an odd bear encounter was misinterpreted. But believers insist only an unknown primate fits Roe's vivid description.

In 1957, Roe drew sketches of the memorable creature under oath to investigators. The images portrayed thick hair covering every inch of the face and body except the chest which Roe described as glossy black skin. And the overall physique aligned with the tapering, non-human shape other witnesses would describe in the Patterson footage a decade later. Roe maintained until his death that no known animal could explain what he saw.

While Roe's incredible sighting preceded the famous 1960s Bigfoot films by over a decade, his detailed testimony matched what Patterson and others would later capture on camera. This lends consistency and credibility that a real creature not yet classified by science inhabited that remote valley. And Roe gained nothing by reporting his bizarre account which he recounted dozens of times without deviation even under oath. In many ways, his story set the template for unknown North American primates generations before the cryptid went mainstream.

Albert Ostman's Abduction Story

In 1957, a Canadian man named Albert Ostman claimed a bizarre incident happened to him 33 years earlier in 1924 when he was abducted by a family of Sasquatch deep in the wilderness of British Columbia. The fantastic tale was met with skepticism when it went public decades later. But Ostman maintained until his death that he was held captive by Bigfoots.

According to Ostman's story, he decided to explore a pristine valley during a solo prospecting trip that was reportedly home to a lost tribe of giants according to local indigenous tales. After trekking for days into uncharted forest, Ostman claims he was startled awake one night in his sleeping bag by a horrendous stench.

Peering out, he saw in the moonlight what appeared to be three apelike creatures hovering over him - two larger ones standing nearly 8 feet tall and a smaller one closer to 5 feet. Before Ostman could react, the largest Sasquatch allegedly lifted him still inside his cocoon sleeping bag and carried him deep into the woods against his violent protests.

Ostman claimed the creatures placed him on the ground somewhere remote then retreated. When he managed to escape from his sleeping bag, he realized he was trapped in a forest basin with the towering beasts occupying the only passage out. With no weapons or provisions, he reluctantly stayed with the Sasquatch family for 6 days until his chance to escape arrived when the giants left temporarily.

Naturally, such a wild tale was met with skepticism when Ostman went public in 1957, 33 years after he claimed it happened. Critics argued no evidence existed like photographs of the valley or the creatures themselves. They also highlight fantastical elements like Ostman helplessly being carried miles away deep into remote woods. Bigfoot proponents counter that Ostman had no motive to fabricate such an account so long after the alleged events. And his detailed descriptions closely matched other witness accounts over the decades.

Ostman maintained until his death in 1975 that he truly spent nearly a week observing a family of relic Gigantopithecus feeding on vegetation and small mammals before plotting his daring escape. His story introduced key Bigfoot behaviors like transporting humans to hidden lairs and communicating through eerie screams. And Ostman noted they possessed a strong stench and left massive prints - details consistent with other reports then and now.

While impossible to authenticate decades later, Ostman's alleged encounter remains an intriguing early account that aligned with both indigenous tales and contemporary witness descriptions. It lent momentum to the argument that an undiscovered bipedal primate does inhabit North America's remote wilds and will go to great lengths to avoid human interactions. Ostman's story stretched credibility but left a tantalizing impression on public imagination that the greatest of apes might still walk among us.

Teddy Roosevelt's Bigfoot Tale

America's 26th president Theodore "Teddy" Roosevelt stands as an iconic adventurer and rugged outdoorsman. But few know that Roosevelt reportedly had a frightening Bigfoot encounter in 1892 according to a little-known tale that surfaced years after his death.

The story stems from Roosevelt's famous 1892 animal-collecting expedition he led in Montana for the Smithsonian Institution. While most know of his chasing western outlaws, the core purpose was scientific - to gather zoological specimens for the nation's museums. This brought Roosevelt deep into the Montana wilderness accompanied by hunters and guides.

According to the account, Roosevelt and two guides were scouting near Hell Roaring Creek when they discovered a fresh Sasquatch kill site - the partially eaten carcass of a grizzly bear suspended in a tree 15 feet off the ground. Alarmed by an animal powerful enough to hoist a bear up a tree, the men retreated to their camp.

But that night, the party was reportedly awakened by the sound of something rummaging through their food supply just outside their tents. Grabbing their rifles, Roosevelt and the guides rushed out to confront a towering Bigfoot creature standing over 8 feet tall next to their ravaged provisions. They opened fire at near point blank range, causing the beast to flee into the darkness with a screaming roar.

The next morning, Roosevelt and his guides apparently tracked the wounded creature's blood trail down to a deep canyon where the trail disappeared into a dark cave. Fearing a confrontation in close quarters, they wisely chose not to pursue the injured behemoth further. The men were so shaken by the incident that they broke camp that same day to retreat from the region in a state of high alert.

Being an election year in 1892, Roosevelt allegedly kept the incident secret to avoid scandal or accusations of exaggeration. The story remained obscure until it surfaced in 1943 when an aged guide named Bauman who claimed to be present finally shared the tale with an author chronicling Roosevelt's adventuring days. Naturally such an incredible account was met with skepticism without further confirmation.

In the end, while Roosevelt's alleged close encounter with Sasquatch seems far-fetched, it also aligns with consistent details in many reports. These include prodigious strength, towering height, unpleasant odor, loud vocalizations, remote forest habitat, and aggression when threatened. Perhaps Roosevelt did indeed cross paths with our wild cousins during his glory days braving the Montana territories. But without corroborating proof, his frightening tale earns a place alongside other pioneering campfire stories from eras when the West remained mysterious and unknown.

The Chilling Ruby Creek Incident

One of the most dramatic early Sasquatch encounter stories involved a group of miners in 1941 who claimed to kill several Bigfoots in self-defense near Ruby Creek, British Columbia. While details remained obscured for decades, the alleged incident lent credence that the beasts roam remote forests and will ferociously defend their territory.

The account stems from a man named John W. Burns who came forward publicly in the late 1990s with a startling tale. He claimed his father, a Canadian miner, told him about a frightening Bigfoot attack that occurred in 1941 deep in the wilds of British Columbia near Ruby Creek.

Burns asserted that his father was part of a small mining team that was suddenly besieged one night by a group of large, aggressive Sasquatch creatures that violently shook their cabin. Fearing for their lives, the miners burst out firing and reported killing at least two of the beasts while the others fled into the darkness. Terrified, the men hastily packed up and abandoned the site the next day.

The incident remained obscure until 1956 when reports surfaced that a Canadian man named William Roe claimed to have encountered several Sasquatch creatures at an abandoned mine near Ruby Creek. This prompted John Burns to contact Roe suggesting they may have discovered the unused cabin where his father's doomed mining friends battled the beasts years earlier.

Seeking answers, Burns traveled to British Columbia to meet with Roe and search for the remote abandoned mine himself. But the exact location still remained hidden. Burns would continue privately researching the incident for decades before finally going public, asserting the Ruby Creek events revealed that Bigfoots will violently defend their territory if encroached by humans.

Naturally such an incredible tale drew skepticism without further evidence. Burns passed away in 2009 but stood by his account until death that his father and several other miners perished in a terrifying 1941 attack by a band of Sasquatch defending the British Columbia wilderness. Believers point to Roe's 1956 sighting as validation something frightening transpired near Ruby Creek.

In the end, with scant records or data, the Ruby Creek incident earns precarious status as an obscure possible explanation for why Sasquatch sightings seem to vanish entirely across certain remote areas. If territorial tribes violently drive out encroaching miners, it could account for pockets of pristine habitat existing free of human interference for decades thereafter. But without more evidence than John Burns' inherited tale, the frightening events remain clouded and unconfirmed. Perhaps the Ruby Creek beasts do still haunt those lonely Canadian mountain slopes, ensuring their sanctuary remains undisturbed to this day.

The Mysterious Bossburg Tracks

In late 1969, one of the most unusual and credible Sasquatch track discoveries occurred near Bossburg, Washington when a series of massive footprints appeared showing one creature walking with a severely injured right foot. Dubbed the "cripple foot" tracks, the set would help validate the existence of Bigfoot through modern dermatoglyphic analysis.

The story began when a Bossburg hardware store owner named Ivan Marx reported finding a set of enormous 16-inch humanoid tracks in the snow along the banks of the Roosevelt River just north of town. The right footprints showed clear injuries with every element distorted and flattened unnaturally. No wildlife could explain the anomaly.

As news spread, investigators confirmed one trackmaker walked bipedally for over 1.5 miles on both dirt trails and pavement, suggesting a 7-8 foot tall, 700 lb creature that intelligently avoided leaving prints on roads where they could be easily discovered. And the pace measured 5 feet between lengthy strides, eliminating bears or shuffle-walking humans. Elk hooves and paws were also easily ruled out.

But it was the crippled right foot that truly confounded experts. Every bone showed unique distortions that would be agonizing for any normal animal. And the matching left prints revealed subtle mid-tarsal flexibility and pressure contours consistent with real anatomy - traits nearly impossible to artificially fake in such fine detail. Skeptics struggled to debunk the tracks as clever hoaxes.

In 1982, famed physical anthropologist Dr. Grover Krantz studied original casts, concluding no known animal or fake could explain the crippled foot's injuries and gait patterns. Using dermatoglyphic analysis, he even matched discernible skin ridge detail between both natural feet and the distorted right track, further authenticating the set as real impressions impossible to hoax given the era's technology.

While the crippled Sasquatch itself was never spotted, its exquisite tracks told the tragic story of a profoundly maimed creature that managed to walk immense distances on horribly-deformed feet while intelligently avoiding interactions with humans. It remains among the most credible Bigfoot trace evidence ever recorded, with skeptics unable to convincingly dismiss the tracks as forgeries even 50 years later. The crippled foot ultimately limped into the mists of mystery, never to be conclusively documented again despite extensive searches of the region.

The Night Siege of Ape Canyon

In 1924, one of the most dramatic alleged Bigfoot encounters occurred when prospectors claimed to be attacked by a group of aggressive Sasquatch while camping in a remote gorge near Mount St. Helens known thereafter as Ape Canyon. The frightening incident lent credence to legends of territorial wildmen willing to defend the Pacific Northwest wilderness against encroaching humans.

That summer, prospector Fred Beck led a small crew into the forests of southwest Washington state near Mount St. Helens in search of gold and adventure. After spotting large, humanoid footprints around their camp, they decided to bed down in a sheltered gorge on the upper flanks of the volcano. But during the night, Beck reported a barrage of heavy rocks suddenly rained down from above as his team fled for cover under their mining equipment.

According to the account, Beck and his crew were besieged throughout the night by rock-hurling Sasquatch that moved stealthily in the darkness, surrounding their crude encampment while letting out unnerving screams, shrieks and howls. The terrified miners sporadically fired shots into the night blindly whenever the creatures drew near. The attack finally ceased at daybreak, allowing Beck and the others to hastily abandon camp.

Newspapers documented that when the shaken prospectors emerged several days later, they brought back plaster casts of massive barefoot prints they discovered ringing their camp - some measuring up to 19 inches long. Authorities who interviewed Beck judged him genuinely rattled by the remote wilderness ordeal. And while physical evidence remains scant today, the Ape Canyon tale lent early credibility that aggressive Sasquatch may inhabit certain Pacific Northwest mountains.

For skeptics, the spectacular story defies belief. They argue no wild animal behaves in such an orchestrated manner nor could the canyon environment enable heavy rocks to be hurled from steep slopes. Bigfoot proponents counter that the unwavering accounts from Beck and his crew closely match other territorial attack reports still occurring today. And the footprints closely resembled those recorded in other remote areas. Without bodies or bones, the reality of events at Ape Canyon remains shrouded in mystery.

In the end, while impossible to conclusively authenticate, the Ape Canyon incident remains an intriguing early account of potential Sasquatch aggression against trespassers. If based in truth, it could explain why certain remote habitats remain devoid of sustained human interference. Much like native tales warning about vengeful wildmen, perhaps the night siege lent truth to legends that Bigfoot creatures violently defend their domains against exploration they perceive as threatening. And if so, they likely still patrol those slopes, hiding just out of view, ready to unleash fury on any reckless enough to encroach too far up the mountain again.

The Prince of Wales Bigfoot Incident

In 1993, a dramatic close range Sasquatch encounter occurred in Alaska's remote Prince of Wales Island between a USDA Forest Service geologist and a Sasquatch that charged within just yards of him. The incident lent further credence that aggressive Bigfoots will defend their territories against perceived threats.

That spring day, geologist Michael Johnson was scouting alone for mineral deposits along a remote mountain stream on Prince of Wales when he detected a foul stench wafting through the air. Scanning the dense brush, he suddenly spotted a huge, hair-covered manlike figure crouching behind some alder trees just 20 yards away.

Johnson described locking eyes with the creature and sensing extreme aggression radiating from its tense posture. As the massive beast rose to stand at over 8 feet tall, Johnson claims he remained frozen in shock when it suddenly charged directly toward him, covering half the distance in just seconds. The terrified geologist finally turned and fled as the pounding footsteps chased after him.

Johnson reported that after running a considerable distance, he paused to look back but saw no sign of the creature. Catching his breath, he swiftly hiked several miles back to base camp, glancing frequently over his shoulder fearing the giant was still in pursuit through the thick woods. But the creature seemed to have disengaged its chase at some point. Still, the frightening close call left Johnson deeply shaken.

When Johnson filed an incident report upon returning from the mountains, his USDA Forest Service supervisors judged his account totally sincere and the visible fear they observed consistent with such an extraordinary ordeal. Experts speculated the creature likely detected Johnson as an encroaching threat near its nesting area and charged in self-defense before ultimately retreating once the perceived risk passed. Such behavior aligns with other accounts of aggression.

While Johnson himself admits he cannot definitively prove what chased him through the Alaskan forest, he remained adamant until his death in 2007 that the creature was no myth - he stared down a real 8 foot tall beast that charged to within frighteningly close range. And USDA authorities did document large, barefoot tracks near where the encounter occurred. Though far from irrefutable evidence, the Prince of Wales incident lent further momentum that Sasquatch creatures still stalk North America's most remote wilds.

The Botched Estes Park Capture

In 1921, one of the earliest organized Bigfoot capture attempts went horribly awry in Colorado's Estes Park valley involving a ranch hand who lured an enormous Sasquatch into a primitive snare only to be gruesomely killed himself during efforts to contain it. The tragic incident lent early credence that capturing a giant wildman was fraught with peril.

According to local newspaper accounts from the era, a cattle ranch foreman named Travis Wilcox undertook the rogue effort to snare a Bigfoot which was reportedly raiding homesteads around Estes Park in the years following World War I. The large, bipedal "mountain devils" as they were known were blamed for mutilating livestock and ransacking food stores. So Wilcox took matters into his own hands and set out to capture one.

After spotting a massive dark, hair-covered creature near his ranch, Wilcox spent weeks strategically baiting it with animal carcasses while gradually constructing a concealed primitive snare trap. Remarkably, the creature finally took the bait, allowing Wilcox to successfully lasso and initially restrain it long enough for him to summon help from nearby ranch hands.

But according to reports, as the men approached what was described as an enormous ape-like beast struggling in the snare, it entered a frenzied rage. The creature violently thrashed about, critically injuring Wilcox by dragging him off his horse and irreparably damaging the restraints. Witnesses claim the mortally wounded Wilcox fired his pistol point blank at the creature before it tore free and disappeared into the forest.

While physical evidence remains scant, a Colorado rancher named John Johnson claimed to have examined the trap site, confirming Wilcox's body as well as damaged ropes consistent with restraining a powerful beast. Johnson even reported sighting two large, hair-covered creatures lurking at a distance through the trees. But by the time law enforcement arrived, only Wilcox's ravaged body could be retrieved.

In the end, while impossible to definitively confirm today, the botched Estes Park capture attempt underscores the extreme dangers of provoking these powerfully violent creatures. It also demonstrates that Sasquatch creatures likely inhabited the Southern Rockies nearly a century before the Patterson film brought Bigfoot into mainstream consciousness. Though the physical proof vanished as quickly as the creature itself, the deadly consequences left behind attest to risks of directly engaging the elusive beasts on anything but their terms.

The evidence

Bigfoot's Footsteps: Analyzing Sasquatch Tracks

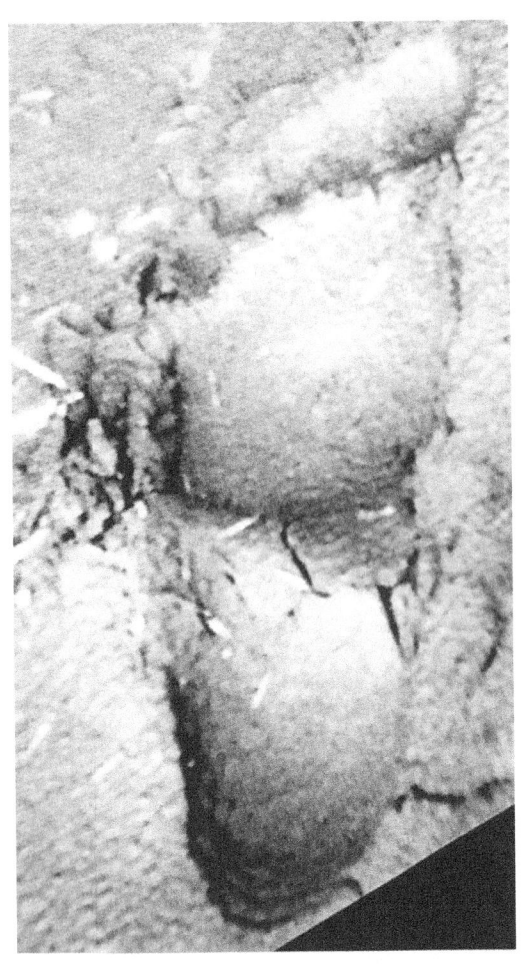

While visual sightings make up the bulk of Bigfoot eyewitness reports, the discovery of inexplicable large footprints comprises some of the most concrete and tangible evidence in the hunt for Sasquatch. Footprints not only confirm the presence of these elusive giants, they offer vital data to deduce anatomy, gait, weight, behavior and more. Noted cases have spawned plaster casts that allow detailed forensic study. By classifying track features, evaluating dermal ridges, pressure points and stride patterns, investigators near scientific confirmation that a giant, undiscovered hominid does indeed stalk the forests of North America.

Famous Cases: Cripplefoot and the Freeman Footage

In the autumn of 2000, logger Paul Freeman discovered a trackway of 16-inch footprints while working in the Blue Mountains of Walla Walla, Washington. The tracks indicated a 7-8 foot tall, 700 lb+ creature walking through the forest. Distinctively, the right foot imprint was badly deformed, reflecting an injury. This "cripplefoot" trackway would reappear repeatedly over the next two years in the same remote area. Plaster casts confirmed the tracks for multiple witnesses, though no sighting occurred. Skeptics claim Freeman hoaxed the tracks himself using custom carved fake feet. But the cripplefoot imprints directly overlapped deer trails through nearly inaccessible terrain, and showed progressive healing of the injury over time. If authentic, the tracks may have belonged to an aging Sasquatch struggling to survive.

The year prior in the Redwoods near Eureka, California, Bob Titmus and other investigators made casts of massive 16 inch tracks crossing a dry creek bed to raid a bait stash of cooked salmon. The elongated, five-toed tracks with distinct dermal ridges matched no known animal. Later examination estimated the creature's height at nearly 8 feet, weighing half a ton. The tracks remain among the most authenticated Bigfoot imprints, though skeptics argue clever hoaxers could carve convincing fake trackmakers. Still, the remote forest location and perfectly distributed pressure points suggest a real 500 lb animal walked through that creek bed. These cases and similar compelling track discoveries spark intense debate about their rightful maker.

Classifying Features

The most credible Bigfoot footprints share key anatomical features setting them apart from known animals. Tracks range from 13 inches to over 22 inches long, wider than a human foot, with five toes including an opposable big toe bearing a triangulated ball. Dermal ridges, pressure points, indentations and abrasions suggest real dynamic foot movement, not rigid fakes. Prints show a mid-tarsal break, reflecting a flexible walking foot adapting uneven terrain. Stride lengths stretch 40 inches or more, denoting legs longer than human proportions. Trails follow obstacle-avoidant natural walking gaits, over broken ground and through underbrush no hoaxer could readily traverse in costume.

Some distinct variations occur regionally, from the wide, short-toed tracks of Texas to the steep-arched imprints of Colorado. Florida's famous Skunk Ape leaves long, narrow, almost delicate footprints compared to the broad, splayed prints across the Pacific

Northwest. This morphological variation may indicate specialized subspecies. But in general, tracks fall into three loose classifications:

- Humanlike: 15-17 inches long, proportioned like an enlarged human footprint.
- Transitional: 17-20 inches long, humanlike shape but larger ball, wider heel, exaggerated arch.
- Ape-like - Over 20 inches, distorted apelike shape, divergent big toe, flat arch.

The most credible tracks show transitional or ape-like proportions exceeding normal human anatomy. Even allowing for hoaxing or errors, these consistent patterns in remote terrain suggest a real creature unlike any known animal.

Examining Dermal Ridges

The best Bigfoot track casts retain clear dermal ridges, the friction lines along foot surfaces unique to each individual like fingerprints. The cripplefoot prints showed dermal ridge detail changing as the injury healed. Leading primatologists like Dr. John Napier and Dr. Jeff Meldrum have analyzed excellent dermal ridge patterns arguing they exceed capabilities of most hoaxers. Napier famously stated, "It is very questionable if fake tracks could be as anatomically convincing as these." Minute analysis of ridges, pores, creases and indentations suggest adaptable, dynamic, flesh-and-blood feet.

However, determined hoaxers like Ray Wallace have used flexible carved wooden trackmakers pressed into soil to yield impressively detailed fake prints later cast in plaster. Both authentic tracks and the best fakes display consistent ridge flow patterns, graded pressure indicating mass and weight, appropriate foot flexibility, and subtle abrasions from forest debris further suggesting a living creature's movement. In the best casts, minute granular detail visible under magnification argues for authenticity, as hoaxing such fine nuances proves extremely difficult in remote terrain.

Stride Patterns and Pressure

Trackways tracing extended Bigfoot movement reveal key clues about gait, speed and weight. Strides often stretch 40-60 inches, reflecting hip joint separation needed to move such a massive body. Length of stride varies with speed, widening faster strides, while stride consistency indicates steady walking pace. The angle of foot placement adjusts with the terrain, reflecting dynamic balance and adaptation. Measuring stride angles helps estimate height by comparing leg length against track separation.

Pressure imprinted also reveals weight distribution. Evenly flattened sole prints suggest extreme mass, while toe dig, heel strike and midfoot pressure indicate flexion and movement. The best fakes can't reproduce these exact pressure nuances outside a studio or lab setting. Pressure mapping of excellent casts like the Skookum Cast yields an estimated weight over 500 lbs, confirming the proportions of a giant biped. Combined stride patterns and pressure imprints produce a profile of height, weight, gait and flexibility that argues for a real animal rather than faked prints though it remains equivocal.

Preserving Authentic Evidence

The most compelling Bigfoot tracks remain those discovered by reputable witnesses in unlikely settings defying easy hoaxing. Rural backcountry locations, deep wilderness, swampy bogs, and steep mountain forests discourage most fakers yet offer prime Sasquatch habitat. Track morphology, dermal ridges, pressure mapping and integrated context like behavior and environmental factors must align to make the most persuasive case for authenticity. As Dr. Meldrum notes, "The proof lies on the footprint itself. The devil is in the details." Careful documentation and expert analysis of excavated prints preserved in plaster casts provide the best hope for making the evidence withstand skeptical scrutiny. While nearly impossible to prove tracks conclusively, science must account for consistent anatomical patterns defying expectations for normal wildlife. As data accumulates across habitats, the footprints suggest a widespread giant hominid does stalk the wilds of this continent, leaving traces of its passing for lucky witnesses to discover.

Dr. Jeff Meldrum's Bigfoot Print Analysis

In the forested mountains of the American West, a scientist searches for traces of a legendary giant. Renowned Idaho State University anthropologist Dr. Jeff Meldrum tracks a tantalizing trail of evidence scattered across the landscape – oversized footprints sunk deep into muddy ground, their dimensions and contours unlike any known wildlife. These mysterious prints capture Dr. Meldrum's imagination and scientific curiosity, leading him to become the world's foremost expert analyzing the potential existence of a giant undiscovered primate – Bigfoot.

Meldrum brings unique expertise to this inquiry as a Ph.D. in anatomical sciences specializing in vertebrate locomotion and evolution. His keen analytical mind, skeptical rigor and expertise in primate foot morphology converge in a decades-long investigation of Sasquatch footprints. Examining dermal ridges, mid-tarsal flexibility, pressure points and more, his findings challenge conventional wisdom by indicating a high likelihood such an unknown species of giant hominid inhabits the forests of North America.

Early Encounters With the Impossible

Meldrum's early work studied primate locomotion in South American monkeys. But a 1993 Walla Walla Union-Bulletin article shifted his focus, describing huge, strange footprints found near Walla Walla, Washington. Intrigued, he interviewed the family who discovered them. Their credibility and emotional intensity piqued his curiosity – the tracks seemed inexplicable by known wildlife. He wondered: could legends of Bigfoot have a factual basis after all? More accounts followed, but scientists largely ignored the implications. Meldrum realized he brought unique expertise to properly assess such evidence. These perplexing footprints became his gateway into cryptozoology.

Meldrum notes as a child in Washington state, "I had heard the stories and imaginings about Bigfoot. It really didn't grab me. But I was always fascinated with footprints." When he moved to southeastern Idaho to take a professorship at ISU, numerous reports from his students compelled him to give the huge footprints serious scrutiny. Meticulous examination convinced him something real lurked behind the local Bigfoot lore. "It just started to add up," he says. "These things can't be explained away. This warranted a closer look."

Analyzing Dermal Ridges & Track Dimensions

Meldrum's analytical strategy brings multiple lines of evidence to bear. He examines dermal ridges, the friction skin detail much like fingerprints. The best fakes can't fully reproduce these minute ridges in floppy costume feet. Their consistent patterns match real weight distribution and foot flexibility. Subtle abrasions and debris further indicate actual walking motion. Meldrum also analyzes proportions, pressure points and stride patterns revealing weight, gait and anatomy. Even skeptics like primatologist Dr. John Napier express difficulty imagining how such tracks could be convincingly hoaxed.

Meldrum made his first plaster cast in 1996, near Walla Walla. The 16 inch long, 7 inch wide, right footprint showed appropriate dermatoglyphics with a visible mid-tarsal break indicating a flexible walking foot. The proportions exceeded human norms, and Meldrum estimated a 7-8 foot tall, 700+ pound creature made it. He realized if authentic, the footprints constituted significant evidence of an unknown bipedal primate. Meldrum began collecting footprint data to quantify Bigfoot's foot morphology, seeking consistency that would strengthen the case for its reality.

Establishing Consistent Anatomy

Careful measurement and comparison of footprint dimensions yielded intriguing anatomical patterns. Length proportions exceed human feet at the same stature by 10%, width dimensions are 15% wider, and they show a splayed, divergent big toe. This data allowed Meldrum to establish a statistical footprint baseline indicating consistent morphology unlike any known species. He eliminated the "giant human" hypothesis popularized by early Bigfoot hunters. If real, this creature possesses a distinct foot structure specialized for its environmental niche.

The most credible tracks show a combination of human and apelike traits, with some regional variation. They indicate an adaptable mid-tarsal flexibility allowing easy walking over uneven terrain by shifting weight side to side. The consistent proportions and pressure patterns can't arise randomly as claimed by skeptics. Meldrum concludes no known natural process or animal creates such uniform foot morphology. Instead, evolution shaped these specialized feet. And the tracks occur widely across North America, coinciding with Bigfoot sighting hotspots.

As his database grew, Meldrum recognized he'd collected a large enough sample to publish serious analytical papers on the tracks without relying on traditional Bigfoot mythology. His first landmark paper appeared in the Journal of Scientific Exploration in 1997, proposing a new hominoid species as the most likely explanation. The response was surprisingly positive, and Meldrum realized many academics shared his view but feared ridicule. His work allowed them to openly agree an unknown primate likely created these tracks. He began speaking at scientific conferences, challenging assumptions and bringing rigorous analytical science to a fringe field, ushering in a new phase of mainstream scientific consideration.

Arguments Against Misidentification

Meldrum's analytical process examines and eliminates every alternate possible explanation before inferring a giant, undocumented ape as the culprit. Careful classification has ruled out hoaxes in remote wilderness contexts, though admittedly clever fakes still occur. Some tracks resemble huge human feet, but dermal ridges, pressure, stride length and gait inconsistencies belie a normal person walking barefoot. No known pathology matches the proportions. Bears leave claw marks and show a flat-footed gait. The splayed toe and mid-tarsal flexibility differs from any known wildlife. While misidentifications happen, a concrete anatomical footprint baseline now exists showing consistent morphology indicating a flesh-and-blood creature.

Bigfoot as a Real Primate

After decades collecting and analyzing data, Meldrum remains convinced a hominid species created these footprints. No other known natural explanation accounts for their consistent appearance over a wide habitat range. "On the basis of footprint evidence," he says, "the presumption is that there is indeed a bigfoot/sasquatch in the northwest forests. The evidence meets the threshold for further scientific consideration." While not irrefutable proof, he considers this evidence far beyond the quality and quantity needed to justify a serious scientific inquiry.

Meldrum's high-profile work legitimizes the search for Bigfoot to mainstream science. Review panels praise his analytical methods and avoidance of speculative pseudoscience even as he challenges entrenched assumptions. His frequent lectures engage both academics and amateurs with thoughtful scientific analysis in this controversial arena. From his unique perspective, Meldrum sees no inherent conflict between rigorous empirical evaluation and examining evidence of seemingly impossible creatures. An open-minded scientific spirit of inquiry drives his ongoing investigations. Only time will tell if his pioneering footprint analysis provides the first step toward unveiling a giant primate unknown to science.

Rover Grantz

Long before Dr. Jeff Meldrum brought mainstream scientific rigor to evaluating Bigfoot evidence, a lone anthropologist at Washington State University blazed the trail. Dr. Grover Krantz, an eccentric but expert physical anthropologist, dedicated years of study towards anatomically classifying these elusive hominids. Ridiculed for his controversial interest in the fringe field of cryptozoology, Krantz was scientifically fearless. He built the first comprehensive models of Sasquatch physiology through forensic analysis of footprints, interpreting sighting reports, and reasoned speculation. His extensive collection of track casts, skeletal models and habitat distribution maps pioneered modern scientific approaches towards identifying Bigfoot as an undocumented ape.

Early Career & Developing Interest

After earning a Ph.D. in anthropology from the University of Minnesota in 1968, Krantz took a professorship at Washington State University teaching courses in human evolution and forensics. His early work focused on Homo erectus and archaeological bone analysis. An avid hiker and wilderness explorer, Krantz collected local Sasquatch lore out of curiosity from his students and communities near his Pullman, Washington campus. Intrigued by the cultural phenomenon more than the validity, he grew fascinated by the regularity of sightings worldwide spanning centuries.

In 1969 he made a cast of huge, strange tracks found near Bossburg, Washington at a remote Native American burial ground. The 16 inch long, human-like prints launched Krantz's scientific investigation of Sasquatch as a real creature. As more reports surfaced, he recognized consistent anatomical patterns underlying the persistent legends. Applying rigorous forensic science, he worked towards a testable hypothesis that an unknown hominid walked the forests of the Pacific Northwest and awaited documentation.

Deriving Anatomy From Tracks

Lacking actual specimens, Krantz used the Bossburg tracks and accumulating casts as his starting point to infer Bigfoot anatomy. Meticulous measurement and analysis of footprint dimensions suggested functional morphology unlike any known ape or human. He noted a flexible mid-tarsal region allowing the foot to contour uneven terrain, combined with a rigid longitudinal arch supporting tremendous weight. Toes showed evidence of grasping ability, while the big toe angled sharply offset from the smaller digits to assist propulsion. Krantz deduced a massive, flexible and stable platform enabling easy travel over rough forest floors.

Estimating the Layered Musculature

Krantz examined dermal ridges and pressure points to model the foot's layered musculature. He envisioned four distinct muscle groups evolved for long-range bipedal travel. Thick distal pads protected force-bearing areas while allowing sensitivity. Tough heel pads stabilized weight, while a thin metatarsal region provided shock absorption and toe flexion. Overall, Krantz deduced a specialized foot structure showing no vestigial ape features – only adaptations facilitating efficient hiking. He calculated stride lengths over 4 feet, suggesting creatures 7 to 10 feet tall. Krantz became convinced Sasquatch evolved as a highly specialized forest-dwelling biped.

Envisioning Size, Shape and Proportions

While acknowledging much guesswork from scant physical evidence, Krantz synthesized a coherent anatomical profile of Sasquatch form, locomotion and lifestyle. He envisioned a barrel-chested creature up to 10 feet tall, weighing over 800 pounds, covered in dark hair excepting the face and palms. Long arms balanced massive shoulders and thick hindquarters housing powerful gluteals. Shorter forearms suggested underdeveloped brachiating muscles, indicating a fully terrestrial adaptation. Krantz modeled the creature's head featuring heavy brows, an occipital bun for massive chewing muscles, and lower positioned ears. He believed female Sasquatches, lacking the male's crest, more easily avoided detection.

Despite criticism for speculating beyond evidence, Krantz insisted deductive logic and forensic reconstruction constituted valid scientific inquiry. As he argued, "You make a hypothesis, and you pursue scientific means to confirm or deny it." He sought to shift discussion towards testable anatomical models subject to eventual verification.

Preserving His Work for Science

In his later years, Krantz focused on preserving his lifetime research for scientific posterity. He collected over 200 track casts along with skeletal models depicting Sasquatch anatomy as he deduced it from prints and sighting accounts. Though rejecting the term "Bigfoot" as too commercialized, he established the scientific basis for understanding these creatures as real biological entities subject to ecological classification. In his final paper published shortly before his death in 2002, Krantz identified the giant sloth as a likely candidate for Sasquatch ancestry over other proposed evolutionary lineages.

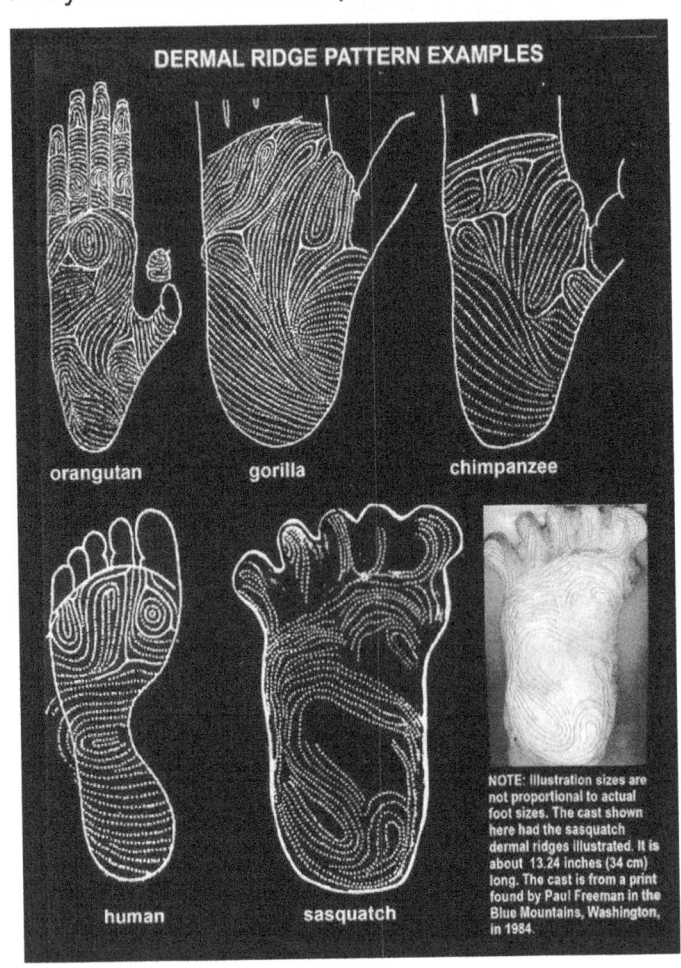

DERMAL RIDGE PATTERN EXAMPLES

orangutan gorilla chimpanzee

human sasquatch

NOTE: Illustration sizes are not proportional to actual foot sizes. The cast shown here had the sasquatch dermal ridges illustrated. It is about 13.24 inches (34 cm) long. The cast is from a print found by Paul Freeman in the Blue Mountains, Washington, in 1984.

Though Krantz's dramatic conclusions drew criticism, his anatomical methods helped establish a basic forensic foundation to build upon. Respected primatologists like John Napier praised Krantz's scientific approach as balanced and rational given the limitations of anecdotal data. Later researchers like Dr. Meldrum adopted his strategy of deducing skeletal structure from isolated tracks. While the controversial Krantz remains a complicated, often polarizing figure, his pioneering scientific analysis lends credibility to the search for an unknown upright-walking primate in the forests of the northwestern U.S. Perhaps, if nothing else, Grover Krantz's daring hypotheses opened the door for others to follow the trail towards one of zoology's final mysteries.

Fur and Hair

Hair and fur samples have long been an intriguing piece of evidence in the ongoing quest to confirm the existence of the elusive Bigfoot creature across North America. For decades, enthusiasts, eyewitnesses, and even some scientific researchers have collected unusual hair samples from remote wilderness areas, hoping they may reveal through DNA analysis that a large, undocumented primate roams the woods. However, the reality of definitively linking hair samples to Bigfoot has proven extremely challenging.

Hair itself contains very small amounts of DNA, making it difficult to extract intact DNA strands for testing. Environmental factors, contamination, degradation over time, and other variables further complicate analysis, sometimes leading to inconclusive or controversial results. Still, a handful of hair and fur samples over the years have provided tantalizing clues that warrant a closer examination. Could these samples provide evidence of a giant, bipedal, humanoid animal?

In this chapter, we will dive deeper into some of the most compelling Bigfoot hair evidence cases. We will explore where samples originated, how they were retrieved and analyzed, and what revelations or new questions the results provoked. The cases range from the famous Patterson-Gimlin film site in Northern California to remote campsites and forests in Oregon, Washington, and beyond.

A common theme across many of these samples is that initial DNA testing only deepens the mystery instead of providing definitive answers. Results often reveal curious mixtures or human DNA intermingled with anomalies that don't match any known species. Inconclusive outcomes typically prompt calls for more sophisticated analyses, specialized laboratories better equipped for challenges hair samples present, and consideration of contamination issues. However, access and funding for such in-depth testing often fizzles out before advocates make much headway.

Extracting and sequencing DNA from hair happens to be very difficult. The shaft of a hair contains no nuclear DNA material - only the root holds viable material for nuclear DNA testing. However, root material is often not present on recovered hair samples. Hair shafts do contain mitochondrial DNA, but the quality and purity of material is frequently poor after exposure to sun, moisture, soil contaminants, etc. The microscopic amount of starting material also hampers laboratory processes for amplifying and copying DNA to detectable quantities.

Contamination poses another complication as hair samples may pick up environmental DNA from other sources like animals and humans. Teasing apart contamination from original DNA is problematic. Preserving chain of custody for hair samples found outdoors proves difficult as well, raising questions later about possible tampering or compromised integrity.

Nevertheless, some hair samples have yielded mitochondrial DNA results suggesting a primate origin. Others align closer to human DNA, but showcase enough anomalies to warrant questioning if genetic markers for an unknown North American primate might reside in the mix. Additional rounds of testing with today's ever improving sequencing technologies could potentially extract more insights from these samples.

What might we expect to learn if an authentic Bigfoot hair sample provided high quality DNA material? We would anticipate locating mitochondrial DNA sequences that branch from ancient primates and evolve onto a distinct path separate from all other hominid lineages. Analysis of nuclear DNA could then reveal genetic relationships linking Bigfoot to other primates as well as unique gene sequences underlying this species' large size, adaptations for wilderness living, or other distinctive traits.

Of course, the reality is that no hair samples to date have enabled such definitive conclusions. Challenges with DNA extraction and sequencing have left nearly all samples in a state of uncertainty without enough clarity to either rule in or rule out a connection to an unknown primate species. Still, the persistence of witnesses and researchers in collecting and studying these enigmatic hair samples suggests they remain one of our best hopes for scientifically proving the existence of Bigfoot. The right samples paired with state-of-the-art DNA technologies could yet yield this elusive creature's genetic blueprint.

The Ketchum DNA Study: A Watershed Moment for Bigfoot Research

In November 2012, a press release sent ripples through the Bigfoot research community, claiming the first comprehensive DNA analysis providing evidence of an unknown North American hominin. The principal investigator behind this groundbreaking study was Dr. Melba Ketchum, a respected veterinarian, scientist, and specialist in animal DNA forensics. Her team's analysis of over 100 DNA samples purportedly originating from Bigfoot creatures pointed to the existence of a human-like species, perhaps the elusive giants countless eyewitnesses across North America have reported seeing for decades.

While mainstream science approached the study with justifiable skepticism, many enthusiasts heralded the results as a major step towards officially recognizing these giants of the forest through genetic verification. Of course, extraordinary claims require extraordinary evidence, and it was only the beginning of a long process to convince the broader scientific community. But Dr. Ketchum's reputation and the study's DNA sequencing data compelled many to give the research an impartial look rather than dismiss it outright based on an unwillingness to challenge long-held assumptions.

The seeds of this study began years earlier with forensic and DNA analysis work Dr. Ketchum's lab performed on anomalous samples from supposed Bigfoot encounters. Intrigued by findings from these early samples, she recognized the potential to apply rigorous scientific techniques to determine if genetic evidence could substantiate the creature's existence. By collaborating with Bigfoot organizations to obtain further samples, she embarked on the first serious DNA sequencing effort carried out by an accredited scientific team rather than amateur enthusiasts.

Over a five-year period, the Ketchum team amassed over 100 hair, blood, saliva, and tissue samples sent by sources claiming to have encountered a Bigfoot firsthand. Rigorous chain-of-custody and documentation standards gave credibility to the origin stories accompanying these samples. Following forensic protocols for eliminating contamination, the study focused solely on samples with the highest reliability of originating from an unknown subject – not just dubious hair samples picked up off the forest floor. Several blood and tissue specimens held particular interest, hinting at rich sources of DNA material.

The study utilized sophisticated DNA sequencing and analysis methods to extract and interpret genetic information encoded in the samples. Mitochondrial DNA provided initial clues of an unusual origin from maternal lineage ancestors. Analysis of nuclear DNA gave a much more detailed profile of genetic sequences compared against known primate genomes. Interpretation required expert analysis and cautious peer review to avoid hastily claiming a new species discovery without ruling out all other possibilities first.

Results proved complex, defying simplistic classification. The unique DNA profiles displayed an intricate mosaic of genetic markers both familiar and unknown. Some markers tied to known primate lineages while others represented genetic sequences never catalogued before in existing scientific databases. Rather than a single "aha" moment of clarity, findings accumulated gradually through a weight-of-evidence approach that this DNA originated from some undocumented North American hominin.

In essence, the DNA analysis ruled out attribution to any species whose genome has been definitively sequenced to date. It also established the samples were not hoaxes or artificial lab creations. That left two broad possibilities - either a new hybrid species or an existing one lacking DNA reference samples for comparison. Most hybrids demonstrate genetic markers from both parent species though, unlike what the analysis revealed. This left the study authors favoring the hypothesis that science has simply overlooked a native North American hominin inhabiting remote wildlands.

From a genetics perspective, the DNA profiles supported categorizing the samples as originating from part of a living population rather than anomalous one-off individuals. And mitochondrial DNA analysis linked this population's ancestral roots to other hominins branching from the primate evolutionary tree at some distant point in the past. Could these samples provide the biological evidence needed to finally acknowledge sightings of a rare North American ape species descended from some shared human-like ancestor?

Upon completion, the Ketchum team looked to publish these groundbreaking results in a peer-reviewed scientific journal, the gold standard for disseminating major research discoveries. However, the study endured rejection after rejection as various publications declined to host such a controversial paper. Critics attacked the research as poorly executed junk science, or even an outright hoax intended to deceive the public. The refusal to publish dimmed enthusiasm for the project in many circles, as lack of peer-reviewed validation gave skeptics more ammunition to dismiss the entire endeavor.

While peer review provides important quality checks for new research, critics noted it also creates barriers for studies challenging entrenched scientific consensus. Negative responses from anonymous reviewers often stem from cognitive dissonance around paradigm-disrupting concepts rather than just technical critiques. Big ideas sometimes encounter hostility before eventually gaining acceptance. The controversy surrounding this study echoed past treatment of new theories like continental drift preceding plate tectonics or H. pylori bacteria causing stomach ulcers.

Unable to find a research journal willing to sponsor proper peer review, the study authors made the controversial decision to publish the paper through an open access journal financed by the study team itself. DeNovo Scientific Journal hosted the publication, though it lacked the prestige of renowned publications like Nature or Science which carry more influence in academic circles. Critics pounced on this self-published route as suspicious, undermining perceptions of the study's legitimacy regardless of the authors' inability to get a hearing elsewhere.

While the unorthodox publication venue opened the door to heightened attacks, the research ultimately needed to stand or fall based on technical merits rather than public relations tactics. Supporters contended that the core methodology and data, not the communication medium, should determine if other scientists view the research as valid, interesting, and worthy of deeper investigation. No journals had published detailed critiques of actual experimental flaws – just condemnations of the study authors' attempts to share findings in alternative ways.

In evaluating DNA evidence for a new species, skeptics often set an unrealistically high bar that specimens must match a pre-existing reference genome closely aligned to Bigfoot descriptions. But requiring such definitive "smoking gun" validation ignores realities of how new species discoveries unfold. The fossil record shows many new species come to light based on a small number of bone fragments, reconstructed from partial data that offers merely suggestive clues until more evidence accumulates over time.

Rather than conclusively proving Bigfoot's existence, the Ketchum study offered tantalizing breadcrumbs for science to follow up on using recently developed forensic and genetic analysis tools. The research community could now re-examine available specimens with fresh perspective thanks to pioneering work laying foundations for others to build upon. As technology continues advancing, the Ketchum team hoped their data might provide base reference points for comparison as more samples emerged that could corroborate the study's findings.

While mainstream science largely ignored the evidence, many ardent Bigfoot researchers heralded this project for breathing new life into the pursuit to validate the creature's existence with physical proof. The study represented a turning point where cryptozoology met advanced DNA sequencing capabilities, elevating discussion beyond just eyewitness sightings and fuzzy photographs. Genetic clues hinted at biology underlying reported behaviors, morphologies, and survival adapted to rugged wilderness sanctuaries.

Further investigation requires open-minded collaboration between credentialed scientists and the grassroots community of Bigfoot devotees collecting samples out in the field. Prior to this study's publication, the scientific establishment largely scoffed at examining genetic traces related to a mythical beast most consider an absurd legend. But Dr. Ketchum's work revealed potentially fruitful new directions for research if taken seriously. A phenomenon that has been part of human history for centuries may yet yield its secrets to those asking the right scientific questions.

The BFRO Hair Samples: Tantalizing Clues and Cautionary Tales

As the world's preeminent research organization investigating sightings of Sasquatch, the Bigfoot Field Researchers Organization (BFRO) fields countless reports each year of large, bipedal, humanoid beasts covered in hair and inhabiting remote forests. Along with collecting eyewitness accounts, the BFRO has worked diligently to catalog physical specimens left behind by these elusive creatures. Hair samples make up one of the largest categories of physical evidence they archive in hopes that scientific analysis may someday confirm a genetic link between the hairs and Bigfoot.

Over decades, the organization has amassed hundreds of hair samples from locations across Canada and the United States where credible Bigfoot sightings have occurred. A few prime samples subjected to microscopy and DNA analysis over the years have yielded intriguing results even if inconclusive. Respected primate researchers and veterinary labs have assisted the BFRO to lend more scientific credibility to evaluating these biological artifacts so tantalizing to enthusiasts seeking evidence of an extant North American ape species.

While the vast majority of samples turn out to originate from known animals after DNA testing, some hairs have presented confusing results matching no known species in wildlife databases. Microscopic appearance and characteristics of mysterious hairs often differ significantly from typical human or animal hair available for comparison. A few singular hair samples have even displayed anomalies suggesting a primate origin, fueling calls for more sophisticated analysis to sequence potential Bigfoot DNA markers.

These outlier results demonstrate why the BFRO continues collecting and investigating even common animal hair samples from areas frequented by giant bipedal creatures fitting Bigfoot descriptions. Witnesses may easily misidentify animal hairs as coming from a menacing monster when discovered in frightening contexts in the woods. Eliminating known animal DNA signatures narrows the pool of samples to focus research efforts on in hopes of eventually isolating true unknowns warranting a Bigfoot link based on genetics.

In the late 1990s, Canadian wildlife officers submitted hair samples to the BFRO that appeared promising as potential Bigfoot evidence. The dark coarse hairs came from multiple remote sites where unusual large prints and massive tree structures suggested a large bipedal creature's presence across central and western Canada. Microscopic examination noted several peculiar characteristics setting the samples apart from typical human or animal hair.

The hairs lacked discernable root bulbs, matched no fur bearing mammals in the region, and showed an unknown pattern of cuticle scale distribution. The scales occurred in groups of five or six and displayed unique variability in shapes, with diamond, flower, and even heart like configurations. Medullary structure also appeared anomalous compared to known wildlife. Finally, the hairs contained an abundance of red pigment granules not seen in bears or normal humans that may signal connections to exotic primates like some New World monkeys.

Intrigued by the highly unusual features noted under microscopy, the BFRO submitted the samples to a Canadian laboratory specializing in animal species identification through DNA testing. However, results showed a genetic match to common native wildlife after all.

Some samples matched wolverine DNA signatures, while others came from deer family species like elk and moose. Though disappointing, this outcome demonstrated the vital role DNA analysis plays in definitively classifying hair samples. Visual microscopic scrutiny alone cannot reliably identify species origin.

In another example, initial microscopic analysis of dark brown hairs discovered after a flurry of Bigfoot sightings in New York state in the early 2000s indicated no match with any species documented in the region. The unknown subject showed a number of anomalies similar to the Canadian samples a few years prior. However, follow up DNA testing traced the hairs back to mammals outside the discovery location - brown bears in one case and domestic cows in another.

The reality that even veteran investigators experience difficulty conclusively identifying species from enigmatic hair samples spotlights the need for genetic analysis. Microscopy provides helpful clues but cannot replace the power of DNA matching for determining if a novel creature or more mundane explanation accounts for mysterious hairs. As much as enthusiasts wish for clear Bigfoot evidence, the vast majority of samples end up originating from common local wildlife after proper laboratory examination.

Through the BFRO's ongoing collection and testing of hair samples, curators have compiled a substantial visual library of microscopic photos serving as a reference database for characteristics of known animal fur. Comparing samples to this resource can help determine if sufficient unexplained anomalies exist to warrant DNA analysis given the time and cost constraints involved. If hair structure, pigmentation, scale patterns, etc. appear fairly normal, genetic testing rarely uncovers surprises.

Conversely, the database also aids in flagging more unusual specimens such as a 2016 sample from Washington displaying traits similar to exotic primates. Intriguingly, DNA tests returned no definitive match to any species on record despite extensive testing by specialized laboratories against global genetic libraries. While not conclusively pegged as Bigfoot hair, the results kept the door open for potential evidence of an unknown primate that further testing could help resolve.

Cautionary tales abound as well demonstrating the propensity for even qualified experts to misidentify out-of-context hair samples. Renowned primatologist Dr. Jeff Meldrum participated in a Discovery Channel documentary analyzing alleged Bigfoot hairs only to discover standard DNA testing traced them to common animals. Microscopy and visual examination again proved misleading without genetic analysis, showing the difficulty even trained professionals have assessing hair samples.

While the vast majority of tested BFRO hair samples have proven irrelevant to Bigfoot evidence once matched to bears, deer, livestock, and other local creatures, the organization still believes collecting biological traces holds value for scientific research. The cases of ambiguous or incomplete DNA results keep hope alive that one day a hair sample with enough intact DNA may reveal genetic markers for an unknown North American hominin.

Mainstream science typically shows minimal interest in analyzing any Bigfoot-related specimens. But the BFRO has productively collaborated over the years with university labs, veterinary researchers, and forensic experts willing to bring an open but critical eye to evaluating such material. Producing multiple peer-reviewed papers lends further credibility to their evidence collecting and analysis protocols beyond what amateur groups can achieve in isolation.

This scientific foundation sets their most unusual hair samples apart from anecdotal eyewitness reports that skeptics easily dismiss as misidentification of known animals or outright hoaxes. Physical samples withstand much greater scrutiny if properly documented with chain of custody showing how materials passed from witnesses through analysis by qualified labs. As DNA sequencing technologies continue rapidly improving, genetic clues in these enigmatic hairs may yet unlock secrets of an elusive ape-like humanoid that science does not currently recognize.

While most evidence ends up supporting mundane explanations, the BFRO knows conclusively eliminating known species brings the research community closer to isolating true biological unknowns warranting attribution to an undocumented North American primate. They compare it to sifting through thousands of grains of sand to uncover a few precious gold nuggets hidden within, unlikely to reveal themselves without first removing distracting debris. Similarly, the quest for Bigfoot requires patient examination of even non-anomalous traces until an extraordinary sample finally provides the breakthrough discovery.

With hundreds of hair specimens archived spanning decades, the BFRO holds hope that persistence will eventually uncover that one-in-a-million Bigfoot hair harboring enough recoverable DNA to sequence genes of a real Sasquatch. Mainstream science may prefer ignoring such evidence in favor of more conventional research. But through collaboration with genetic and forensic experts, the BFRO knows proven collection and analysis protocols give credibility to evaluating biological samples with the scientific rigor needed to make new species discoveries.

So while the vast majority of hair samples turn out unremarkable under the microscope or DNA sequencer, they still provide pieces to the puzzle through a process of elimination. Identifying local wildlife tells researchers where NOT to concentrate efforts while highlighting peculiar genetic outliers for further inquiry. Somewhere in the BFRO archives may already rest the microscopic evidence that could reshape our understanding of North American hominin evolution.

Hair Samples from the Enigmatic Skookum Cast

In September 2000, a landmark piece of potential Bigfoot evidence surfaced in the remote Gifford Pinchot National Forest of Washington state - a large impression left in the ground along with hair samples recovered at the discovery site. Dubbed the "Skookum Cast" after the Skookum Meadows area, the impression recorded a large figure apparently reclining on the ground, leaving behind the smooth earth mold of a hairy flank and appendages resembling a buttock, thigh, arm, and lower leg. Hairs collected from plants and soil around the body imprint spotlit another avenue for identifying what sort of large, hairy creature made itself comfortable in the wilderness, shedding hairs that would baffle investigators for years to come.

The initial Skookum expedition in 2000 had followed up on local sightings of very large, bipedal, hair-covered beasts trekking through the remote area in recent years. Tribal histories described such creatures, known as Seatco, inhabiting the region's forests for centuries. Reports from local Bigfoot enthusiasts pointed the researchers to a specific meadow where they set up a night watch in hopes of glimpsing one of the elusive giants.

What they discovered the next morning would prove far more remarkable and controversial than a fleeting sighting. Right in the midst of thick ferns and brush, an impression measuring nearly seven feet long by three feet wide marked a distinct body-shaped indentation. The smooth, compacted soil evidenced something massive reclining and pressing down vegetation in that spot. Plaster casts made of the impression recorded the mysterious figure's contours, revealing provocative hints of a large, muscular animal with proportions quite unlike any known local wildlife.

Could it have come from one of the secretive Seatco giants numerous witnesses claimed to see traipsing through these remote North Cascades slopes? If so, photographs showed the partial body print bore an uncanny resemblance to descriptions of the region's Bigfoot creatures. Beyond the compelling impression itself, the discovery scene held further clues in the form of coarse dark brown and red-tinged hair strands caught on branches, twigs, and ferns fringing the immediate area.

The hair evidence proved especially tantalizing. Initial microscopic analysis revealed multiple distinguishing features that did not match typical properties of regional mammals. Scale patterns, pigment granules, shaft form, and transparency differed markedly from known animals. The investigation team felt confident eliminating black bears, deer, elk, cougars, wolves, and all other fur bearers indigenous to the region as potential sources of the unusual hair strands. Intriguingly, certain characteristics observed aligned closer with primate hair, though no apes or monkeys inhabited anywhere near this Pacific Northwest forest.

These initial findings at the discovery site already added credence to the possibility that the body imprint resulted from a mysterious unrecognized creature, perhaps even lending evidence to the Bigfoot hypothesis. But more detailed scientific examination of the hair samples and surrounding soil would be needed to rule out all standard explanations before asserting a claim as extraordinary as proof that these Sasquatch-like beings indeed roam Washington's forests. In the ensuing months and years, ensuing waves of analysis sought to shed further light on whether an unknown beast could have left behind the enigmatic Skookum traces.

Zoologist Dr. Henner Fahrenbach conducted in-depth hair analysis, noting several features consistent with primate fur as well as some unusual traits rarely seen. Though unable to conclusively classify the samples as Bigfoot hair, he felt comfortable stating they matched nothing commonly found in the region. Environmental DNA survey work also checked for genetic traces of known animals across the discovery site without success. Soil structure examinations revealed the impression resulted from weight and pressure rather than dug out manually.

All evidence continued pointing to something quite anomalous pressing down at the location, becoming partially molded and shedding coarse hair strands. But what creature could have produced this scene so confounding to wildlife experts? Primate origins seemed unlikely this far from tropical habitats, yet no other species explanations made sense either. Though much analysis ensued on the body cast itself, the hair samples presented their own mystery that scientific teams struggled to crack.

Most Sasquatch observers describe a tall, broad-shouldered, hairy bipedal animal walking on two feet. The chance to directly analyze physical samples possibly coming from such a being represented a rare opportunity to look for biological evidence underlying the Bigfoot phenomenon. Hairs shed from an unknown forest giant could open the door to

DNA analysis revealing evolutionary origins, relationships to other primates, anatomical adaptations, and more insights about these elusive creatures.

Accordingly, the original Skookum expedition leaders sought out genetics labs willing to sequence DNA from hair shafts and follicles collected on site. Early results hinted at a confusing mixture of genetic material from common wildlife along with unidentified components. Concerns emerged that surface contamination or incomplete DNA isolation in the testing skewed initial interpretations. The samples required higher resolution laboratory analysis to carefully parse environmental contaminants from original genetic signatures.

However, this more sophisticated DNA work required funding support that proved challenging to sustain long term. As the years passed, the strange Skookum Cast continued causing ripples in Bigfoot circles but scientific curiosity around the hair samples waned. Without an institution willing to prioritize advanced genetic sequencing costs, the early DNA work stalled out. But technology has progressed tremendously since 2000, reigniting hopes that new testing could yet extract usable DNA to help identify what sort of forest giant might have reclined in that meadow.

Researchers speculate improved analysis may yet yield mitochondrial DNA evidence signaling a relation to ancient primate lineages. Nuclear DNA markers could also reveal genetic relationships linking the Skookum hair samples to other primates as well as novel gene sequences specific to these giants. Bigfoot enthusiasts imagine one day having conclusive DNA confirmation that Sasquatch-type families have long roamed North American forests as the ultimate vindication by science.

Of course, many questions linger about whether suitable hair samples exist in this case to provide enough high quality genetic material for definitive DNA analysis after two decades. But with ever advancing sequencing capabilities, researchers hold out hope that revisiting these enduring biological artifacts from the perplexing Skookum scene could yet crack the genetic code of this mysterious fur-covered hominin.

Even if not clearly pegged to Bigfoot by DNA testing, the inability to tie the Skookum hair samples to any known local animal keeps the door open to something unexpected wandering the deep woods. Mainstream biology has documented over 20 new mammal species in the Pacific Northwest just since the influential Skookum Cast discovery in 2000. Could a rare, reclusive bipedal primate have left its subtle traces by briefly bedding down on the forest floor that September night so many years ago?

The unidentified hair samples still seem to tell a tale that no common explanation fully satisfies. And with the passing years, the remarkable body impression left behind looks more and more out of place juxtaposed against native wildlife activity. The original investigators' conviction remains steadfast that an incredible discovery took place in those remote Washington meadows two decades ago. It just may take today's scientific tools and open-minded thinkers to finally decipher the secrets encoded in strands of hair shed by one of the region's most legendary beasts.

Bigfoot vocalizations and sound recordings

Bigfoot Encounters Are Not Silent Events

Eyewitness accounts of Sasquatch creatures often describe unsettling noises and strange vocalizations accompanying sightings of these large, bipedal, humanoid beasts. While fleeting visual glimpses create the starkest impressions for those who encounter North America's most famous cryptid, soundscapes surrounding these events prove equally intriguing. Reported incidents consistently feature prominent audible components - from loud crashes indicating heavy footsteps, to wood knocking signaling territorial markers, to frightening screams expressing aggression. Taken together, vocalizations and structural sounds potentially originating from Bigfoot beings help round out the context for understanding their presence in certain locations.

This chapter dives deeper into the audio side of Bigfoot eyewitness reports by cataloging notable sound types these creatures purportedly produce. We explore current theories around the purpose and mechanics behind vocalizations like screams, howls, whoops and other outbursts. Structural behaviors like wood knocking or rock throwing demonstrate additional means for Sasquatches to generate noise in their remote forest environments. Various recording efforts over decades attempt to document these sounds as further proof that large, undiscovered hominins dwell in the wilds of North America.

While most reported vocalizations cannot be definitively attributed to an unknown primate versus more prosaic forest animals, some stand out as exceptional and difficult to ascribe even to known species. Recordings of exceptionally loud screams from remote areas of Michigan's Upper Peninsula attracted the attention of wildlife biologists surprised at their volume, pitch variability, and durability over repeated sequences. The 1982 recordings first popularized theories of an unknown hominin in the region amongst locals who referenced a large, loud creature called the "Michigan Monkey Man." Other recordings of high pitched wails from remote forest locations like this continue fueling debate around what sort of animal - or humanoid beast - could produce such disturbing shrieks.

Bigfoot screams and howls feature prominently in sighting reports from every region these creatures reportedly inhabit. Witnesses consistently describe vocalizations as piercing, preternaturally loud, traversing significant distances, and projecting an eerie, otherworldly feel unlike any normal forest creature. Some report physical effects from the auditory onslaught too - headaches, nausea, or dizziness from the cacophony. Whether infrasound components produce such effects or sheer loudness alone remains untested given the lack of clear Bigfoot call recordings available for acoustic analysis.

In many audio recordings, vocals do not follow expected biological models - exhibiting no tapering at onset or conclusion as most animal calls do. Instead they show instantaneous initiation and cut off more akin to human shouts. This anomaly fuels ongoing debates whether Sasquatch screams originate from actual animals or hoaxers employing electronic devices or human collaborators. Some theorists even speculate on a psychic component or form of mimicry underlying inexplicable attributes of sounds attributed to these mysterious creatures. Without a verified Bigfoot recording, the vocalization debate continues.

Besides piercing screams, Bigfoot encounters also regularly include knocking sounds made by striking wood against trees or rocks together to produce loud, carrying percussion able to traverse significant distances across remote forests. These wood knocks often occur in structured sequences - commonly described as three successive hits followed by silence and repetition. Witnesses observe this pattern continuing for hours as if the knocker slowly circles the location.

This behavior strongly indicates a signaling function, though what message gets conveyed remains unclear. Leading theories suggest wood knocking demarcates territorial boundaries to warn others of the knocker's presence much like how gorillas beat their chests. Some researchers also speculate knocking may represent a form of communication between multiple creatures. Analyses of wood knock acoustics indicate exceptional capabilities for producing resonance and projection far beyond typical human percussion.

Whoops, howls, whistles and other vocalizations further expand the sound repertoire witnesses attribute to Sasquatch creatures across reported habitats. Observers consistently comment on the wide pitch variability, unusual textures, and exaggerated loudness compared to known species. Recordings showcase everything from deep, grunting roars to high, keening wails traversing remarkable frequency ranges and transitioning instantly across octaves without gliding.

Bigfoot sounds hold enduring fascination due to their departure from expected biological models. Expert analysis indicates lung capacities, vocal fold anatomy, and articulatory capabilities outside the range of documented terrestrial mammals. While some primate traits do get exhibited, inconsistencies and extreme parameters defy conclusions that known species alone can account for these vocalization patterns. Something with more advanced sound production anatomy seems required - intriguing evidence for a large, undiscovered hominin.

The context of sounds also adds significance when evaluating origins. Remote forests and mountainous regions far from human habitation provide ideal conditions to record and study mysterious vocalizations without interference. Documenting an unknown creature's natural soundscape paints a richer picture of its behaviors and interactions with environments devoid of human influence. Sounds give researchers clues about the secret lives of these elusive beings.

Recordings from Michigan to California have yielded samples defying easy categorization as common wildlife, accumulating into a compelling body of evidence that mysterious creatures populate North America's forests. Ongoing recording initiatives driven by both amateur enthusiasts and PhD scientists aim to definitively document vocalizations from secretive, hairy, humanoid beasts that eyewitnesses continue to encounter.

This chapter will survey some of the most notable Bigfoot scream recordings and analyze what insights their sonic signatures reveal around lung capacity, pitch range, articulation, and other anatomical features. We assess current evidence on structural knocks and other sound production behaviors attributed to these enigmatic creatures. And we explore what the evolution of reported vocalization data could mean for substantiating a rare North American hominin that science does not yet formally recognize

The Sierra Sounds: Window into a Hidden World

Few pieces of evidence spark more controversy or intrigue in the Bigfoot world than the Sierra Sounds - a collection of bizarre vocalizations recorded in California's Sierra Nevada mountain range during the 1970s. For decades, these audio samples have fueled endless debate over their origin and meaning. Believers argue the recordings capture a Bigfoot language, revealing the creatures possess advanced communication abilities. Skeptics hear nothing but people imitating animal noises. Yet even harsh critics struggle to definitively identify the vocalizer or dismiss why certain qualities defy biological explanation.

The story behind the Sierra Sounds begins in the early 1970s with aspiring Bigfoot researchers Ron Morehead and Alan Berry. Camping in Sierra remote wilderness, hoping to glimpse the elusive creature, they instead captured a series of strange sounds on tape that would shock later listeners. Their audio library swelled over months until relocating for work ended the nighttime recording vigils. But the unique vocal collection they amassed continues inspiring new generations of Sasquatch devotees.

Returning from one trip, Berry played the tapes for a local journalist acquainted with indigenous people of the region. She immediately asked - "why do you have recordings of Native American ceremonies?" This seemingly odd reaction actually supported the sounds' authenticity. Local tribes described "hairy mountain people" inhabiting the same remote wilds where Berry and Morehead taped the calls. Perhaps these recordings did echo vocal rituals of an unknown forest tribe.

In the nearly 50 years since, the Sierra Sounds have been cited, played, and debated more than any other Bigfoot evidence aside from the Patterson-Gimlin film. Believers hear the vocalizations as potential proof these creatures possess advanced language and speech abilities rather than just simple animal calls. Analyses by specialists in linguistics, primate communication, and audio engineering reveal unique qualities unlike any wildlife while still matching patterns that could signal rudimentary syntax or conversation flows if originating from humanoid beasts.

The most vocalizations occur on an evening in September 1971 after Berry and Morehead's campfire apparently attracted something's attention. What unfolds is a cacophony of shrieks, growls, and guttural barks punctuated by heavy footsteps circling their campsite. But more remarkable are interspersed sequences featuring intricate vocal patterns clearly responsive to one another's calls. These two distinct sound types have been dubbed Samurai Chatter and the Baby Cry by enthusiasts awed by their lifelike, almost human-esque emotionality.

The Samurai Chatter includes perhaps two dozen vocalizations over three minutes - deep, resonant growls rhythmically modulated from bass to tenor tones in looped sequences that rise and fall like chanting warriors. Rough textures suggest extremely wide vocal cavity dimensions far surpassing human anatomy. Sound engineers describe traits no known species exhibits, like instant amplitude leaps across three octaves without transitional gliding. Morehead himself turned hoax accuser until conceding no wildlife or special effects could mimic such otherworldly sounds.

Meanwhile, the Baby Cry disturbs listeners with its uncanny resemblance to a human infant wailing. Its shrill, warbled quality tugs heartstrings with what seems a clear emulation of sadness or grief. Primate researchers describe innate universal cues that suggest a juvenile in distress. It stands apart from the rest of the Sierra Sounds as perhaps the most anthropomorphically emotive sample in the entire Bigfoot vocalization canon.

Understandably, many dismiss the entire Sierra Sounds collection as an elaborate hoax. Critics highlight that no Bigfoot evidence definitively confirms these creatures' existence, so assuming the recordings as proof of their advanced communication abilities makes little sense without first establishing basic biology. They also emphasize the long history of pranksters imitating wildlife and monster sounds to fool others all too eager to believe without proper skepticism.

However, serious analysis lends some credibility to the samples' authenticity even if absolute proof remains lacking. Morehead and Berry documented discovering large, humanlike footprints surrounding their campsites corresponding to the nights such vocal activity occurred. This helps counter the usual accusation of friends simply hiding in the woods making animal noises as a joke. Trackway evidence indicated a substantial creature - whether prankster or actual beast - moving about as the sounds commenced.

Sound engineers also express doubts that 1970s recording equipment and conditions could capture vocalizations so cleanly and evenly across a wide pitch range under outdoor nighttime forest conditions. Mimicking certain non-biological audio traits so perfectly and consistently seems unlikely for amateurs trying to hoax monster noises. The ambient signature of natural remote environments gets retained in the recordings, not the echo or flatness of studio production.

Of course, other experts posit plausible mainstream explanations for the sounds involving known species combined with illusion of meaning projected onto meaningless noise by overeager listeners. Pareidolia tendencies in human psychology could make scattered animal calls seem structured or responsive when they happen to overlap by coincidence. But this fails to address some of the more anomalous vocal attributes defying clear zoological classification.

Seeking clearer resolution, Morehead and Berry allowed analysis by world-renowned bioacoustics pioneers including the late George Witteveen and the late R. Lynn Kirlin. Both specialists described vocals exceeding expected lung and vocal tract capacities for any documented terrestrial mammal. They also noted distinct audible patterns not occurring randomly as expected for wildlife calls. Could more advanced sound production anatomy be required if the recordings have natural biological origins?

In the 1990s, a Sylvanic language theory emerged proposing that nuanced inflections, pitches, and rhythms embed communicative meaning - perhaps representing a primitive conversation between multiple creatures. Linguists note apparent sentence structure and responsive exchanges rather than just animalistic noise. Believers speculate on a language ability allowing Sasquatches to coordinate sophisticated group behaviors for survival success despite reclusiveness.

Mainstream biology rejects implications of advanced cognition and language for undiscovered hominins in North America. But witness accounts over centuries report meaningful gestures, signaling, and responsive interactions with these forest giants, hinting at greater intelligence than a mere brute animal. Recordings like the Sierra Sounds lend credibility to such observational anecdotes if their vocal patterns reflect higher brain functionality.

For decades, the Sierra Sounds endured as the best available but inconclusive evidence of Bigfoot language abilities. But the early 2000s discovery of a new vocalization collection in Washington's Cascade Mountains sparked renewed interest in studying recordings of these elusive creatures. The Salish Sea Sounds featured similarly bizarre vocals with even more conversational-like exchanges. Some call it the Rosetta Stone for decoding a potential Northwest forest language that linguists can finally parse by comparing multiple recording locations.

Most Sasquatch observers describe vocalizations as just one aspect of dynamic communication abilities also involving wood knocking, gestures, and body language. Knocks and gestures seem to precede vocal exchanges in some reports, suggesting integrated messaging modes. Recordings alone cannot capture these broader behavioral contexts, but they showcase tangible sound samples for analysis unlike the ephemeral nature of sightings.

Recordings allow continuous re-examination as technology improves to tease out new insights on anatomy, acoustics, language patterns, and meaning. Over 50 years later, the Sierra Sounds still present an alluring puzzle - biological or synthetic origin? Animalistic noise or structured conversation? With advanced analysis and comparison to new recordings potentially forthcoming, perhaps the clues embedded in these vocal sequences will yet reveal secrets of their enigmatic makers hiding just out of sight amongst North America's remote wildernesses.

A Navy Codebreaker Cracks the Case

In the decades following the Sierra Sounds recordings that first catapulted Bigfoot vocalizations into public imagination, the audio samples endured as the most hotly debated piece of potential Sasquatch evidence aside from grainy films showing fleeting glimpses of giant bipedal beasts lumbering through forests. Believers heard the Sounds as proof these creatures possess advanced communication abilities and language skills rather than merely making animalistic noises. Skeptics argued witnesses likely misinterpreted calls from known wildlife or that pranksters staged an elaborate hoax. The recordings alone could not seem to provide sufficient context to sway opinions in either direction.

That stalemate endured until the early 2000s when a new player entered the fray - former U.S. Navy cryptolinguist Scott Nelson. His codebreaking work for Naval Intelligence commanded immense respect decoding Russian communications across multiple channels. Nelson also taught at the Navy's prestigious cryptologic school honing new linguists' skills. If anyone could potentially crack the Sierra Sounds mystery from an informed linguistic perspective, Nelson seemed an ideal candidate.

Upon first hearing the vocalizations, Nelson felt immediately intrigued by their apparent structured patterns - reminiscent of his Navy experience deciphering meaning from foreign communications. Though fascinated by the Bigfoot phenomenon for years through his wife's Native American heritage, Nelson initially joined the skeptic camp in assessing these controversial recordings. But the more time he spent analyzing the Sierra Sounds, the more convinced Nelson became that discernible language elements suggested a speaker far beyond known wildlife.

In his initial report released in 2004, Nelson lays out a compelling case for what he deems definitively constitutes structured linguistic content embedded within the vocal sequences. First, he emphasizes how patterns emerge through careful parsing that no known natural species exhibits in its calls. The flow follows recognizable "sentence" components - initial call, pause, repeat, secondary rejoinder, pause. He asks listeners to imagine substituting words for vocalizations to recognize this as a rudimentary conversational exchange.

Nelson further notes how certain calls only occur preceding or following other specific calls - suggesting meaningful symbolic relationships where order matters, unlike randomly scattered animal noises. He also highlights distinct regional dialects across separate Sierra Sounds recording locations just miles apart. Such nuanced local inflections would seem highly improbable for any common wildlife species roaming the entire region.

In contrast, subtle dialect variations fit perfectly with extended family clan groups maintaining seasonal territories generation after generation. Nelson suggests hard science must acknowledge that multiple lines of evidence point toward structured language capabilities no modern ape possesses, but which a bipedal hominin could conceivably retain in isolation. He admits a level of interpretation enters his analysis but emphasizes that context offers the strongest case for assessing credibility of any claim.

Ultimately, Nelson concludes only acceptance of an undocumented species inhabiting North America can account for the full suite of anomalies he meticulously details in structural analysis of the Sierra Sounds. He challenges fellow scientists uncomfortable with such an extraordinary claim to provide more logical alternative hypotheses for the recorded vocals' linguistic qualities and conversation-like characteristics. No plausible explanations forthcome aside from an unknown hominin speaking some primitive forest language.

Nelson further builds on his Sierra Sounds analysis by examining recent advances in great ape language studies, including the famous case of Koko the gorilla mastering American Sign Language. He highlights research showing apes capable of comprehending sentence structure, symbolic representation of objects, and intentional modification of word order to alter meaning. If less advanced gorillas demonstrate this language groundwork, Nelson argues a more evolved North American hominin could surely develop higher functional linguistics.

He notes that Sasquatch creatures split from other great apes millions of years ago if the species proves valid. Extended evolution in small tribal clusters through changing ice ages and environmental pressures could prompt more complex communication than their tropical cousins require. Isolated mountain habitats blocking migration would also allow prolonged language system stability - unlike mixed populations diluting dialects.

Nelson concludes by lamenting that scientific disdain for considering Bigfoot evidence prevents proper evaluation of his linguistic analysis. He pleads for intellectually honest assessment based on recording merits and pattern data alone without stigma over origins. If nothing else, the Sierra Sounds objectively demonstrate non-random signaling unlikely in known wildlife. By listening closely through a communications lens, Nelson believes clues emerge exposing a rudimentary forest language and North America's most elusive beings.

Reactions to Nelson's Sierra Sounds study spanned the gamut from awed excitement to harsh dismissal. Bigfoot believers heralded his naval cryptography credentials in lending legitimacy to theories about advanced language capacities. His pattern analysis and dialect arguments provided them scientific cover to counter skeptics always demanding more "proof" before taking the species possibility seriously. Nelson's stature made him harder to dismiss as some amateur crackpot chasing mythical monsters.

Other linguists also praised Nelson's analytical approach to decoding possible language structures by diagramming call type sequences. They welcomed introducing communications analysis methods into cryptozoology for more rigorous evaluation of anomalies like the Sierra Sounds recordings defying easy categorization. Even if Nelson's interpretations later proved unsupported, his techniques helped strengthen the methodology toolkit available to analyze such evidence.

Critics focused their attacks on Nelson's limited peer review, small sample size from just one region, and charges that he fell prey to pareidolia tendencies causing apophenia seekers to perceive patterns in meaningless noise. Some chastised his Navy background as undermining objectivity on a question requiring zoological expertise. Without formal training in primate communications, how could Nelson justify claiming discovery of a heretofore unknown hominin language?

Skeptical linguists further highlighted the lack of consensus in Nelson's field that any great ape vocalizations definitively constitute true language with syntax and grammar. If the primate communication question remained unsettled after decades of study, they argued no evidence supported the extraordinary claim that secretive Bigfoot creatures somehow acquired advanced linguistics. Nelson's pattern analysis failed to clear the burden of proof required for such an outrageous proposition.

Ultimately, the clash of opinions following Nelson's work echoed long entrenched positions around treatment of Bigfoot evidence in general. Those leaning toward acceptance felt he presented a reasonable probability case for the Sierra Sounds potentially indicating language capabilities hitherto unproven in the scientific arena. Critics saw only speculation wrapped in an aura of credibility from his otherwise distinguished naval career. The same recordings spawned radical disagreement over analysis and conclusions.

However, Nelson raised difficult questions around explaining the Sierra Sounds through known biological models that skeptics struggled to conclusively resolve. If not hoaxed and not attributable to any recognized species, what could possibly account for vocalization patterns notable enough to captivate a cryptography expert? Even harsh critics failed to provide alternative hypotheses matching Nelson's interpretive depth from a structured communications perspective.

While the language question remains hotly contested, Nelson made lasting contributions to how Bigfoot vocalizations get studied. By documenting pattern analysis methodologies, he enabled more systematic evaluations for signals potentially indicating meaning or intent. He set precedents that recordings required much closer analytical scrutiny with an open mind to the possibility that persuasive evidence already exists in long marginalized audio samples like the Sierra Sounds. And Nelson's naval codebreaking background demonstrated that highly skilled communications specialists can still acknowledge profound mysteries worthy of deeper exploration rather than reflexive dismissal.

A 'nest' by a Russian yeti

Bigfoot Nests and Shelters

One compelling piece of anecdotal evidence for the existence of Bigfoot are the large, intricate nest structures occasionally discovered deep in remote forests. These mysterious constructions, thought by some to be the handiwork of Sasquatch, showcase engineering abilities and survival instincts consistent with a highly intelligent great ape.

In this chapter, we will analyze the key characteristics of these nests, their geographic distribution patterns, similarities to shelters built by other primates, and what they may reveal about the elusive creature behind them.

Discovery and Locations

Bigfoot nests have been uncovered across much of the Pacific Northwest region of North America, with a concentration of sightings in the dense temperate rainforests found there. Areas like the Redwood forests of Northern California, the Cascade Mountain Range extending through Oregon and Washington, and the coastal forests of British Columbia, seem to produce more nest findings than other parts of the continent.

One reason may be the lush ecosystem and abundant food sources available to sustain a small population of large primates. Some experts also point out that the rainfall and vegetation coverage in these coniferous and redwood forests allow Bigfoot to remain concealed and construct their shelters easier. An examination of nest locations reveals they are found most frequently near streams, ponds or swampy areas, suggesting Bigfoot may prefer wetter habitats.

The first documented discovery occurred in Washington state in 1970, by a group of hikers who came across an 8 foot tall domed structure made of interwoven branches and sticks that was clearly not the work of humans. Since then dozens more have surfaced, with two separate nests found recently in 2021 in the same area of Utah's American Fork Canyon.

Construction and Composition

In their structures and composition, Bigfoot nests share similarities but also display key differences setting them apart from the work of any other native animal. Common traits include:

- Large size – 7 to 15 feet across, with nest interior up to 8 feet high, requiring branches 20+ feet long
- Domed or tepee shape, formed by leaning long branches together then interweaving smaller sticks and vegetation
- Bent and broken branches used as structural supports more than chopped or torn ones
- Located high up in trees or on steep hillsides, as if for protective concealment
- Often incorporate parts of existing trees and incorporate natural debris from the forest floor
- Contain bedding material such as pine needles, leaves, bark and moss

The scale of these nests alone excludes nearly any other wildlife native to the habitats they are found in. Black bears construct nests for winter hibernation, but those max out around 5 feet in diameter using small broken branches and leaves, without structural reinforcement capable of supporting a 500+ pound Sasquatch.

Other similarities exist to the work of the mountain gorilla of Central Africa. Groups have been observed building rudimentary night nests by bending and snapping off vegetation, and these nests being reused multiple times. This hints at a knowledge of construction passed down genetically and through learned group behavior, as opposed to pure instinct seen in bird nest building.

If built by Bigfoot, certain questions arise. Are new nests built for overnight shelter while on the move, or do certain nests function as more permanent base camps, perhaps for small family units? Is there evidence of nest reuse over time? What can we deduce about group travel sizes based on number and size of nests in an area? Unfortunately the sparse data on nest structures leaves many questions open.

Clues About Bigfoot Behavior

Beyond tangible construction, these nests may offer intangible clues to Bigfoot behavior patterns if indeed built by these mysterious creatures. As with any wild animal, an understanding of habits can aid in location and observation in their natural habitat.

The locations are informative - dense forest with plenty of tree cover, ample fresh water sources nearby, and abundant vegetation and wildlife to sustain foraging needs. Proximity to ponds, marshes and streams also provides mud and clay for another theory: that Bigfoot use certain plants and natural minerals to treat illnesses or wounds.

These nests suggest a creature strongly adapted to forest living, not unlike our ancestors transitioning from the African savannahs to areas like the Siberian woodlands of Russia and the Pacific Northwest. In fact, the Russian Almas legends refer to wild people and their cone-shaped tree nests.

The nests also display evidence of basic tool use - the bending and breaking of branches to form structural beams. While no stone tools or weapons have been found, this shows an elementary construction technique. And while birds and apes build nests purely on instinct, these appear to show progressive learning feats. Combined with fire starting and rock throwing, the case is made for an intelligent builder.

Of course, the biggest question is why no Bigfoot bones, fossils or bodies have been reliably found. Skeptics argue that regardless of legends or modern sightings, a large undiscovered ape in North America would have left behind some tangible remains. Believers counter that the wildness and seclusion of these creatures mean they know how to hide themselves, including the dying who feel that instinct to withdraw deep into the forest. And in the case of bones, the acidic soil of the Pacific Northwest quickly breaks down calcium, leaving no fossils behind.

Such structures, often reported by hikers and researchers in remote woodlands, are thought by some to be territorial markers, navigational aids, or even forms of communication among these cryptic creatures.

rare offshoot branch of Gigantopithecus, Paranthropus, or other prehistoric ape adapting to the New World? Or is there a more mundane explanation waiting to be discovered? For those who study the enigma of Bigfoot, they serve as yet another clue in the search for more definitive proof. Perhaps the future will reveal if these impressive creations are the work of man, beast, or something in-between.

Tracking Bigfoot Home: The Olympic Project Nest Discovery

In the dense, remote rainforests of Washington's Olympic Peninsula, a hotbed of Bigfoot sighting reports and lore, a dedicated team of researchers explored off-trail in hopes of making new discoveries in 2013. Unlike most enthusiasts pursuing fleeting sightings or recordings, the Olympic Project organized scientific field work to uncover tangible physical evidence of these elusive beasts. Strategically searching for signs of habitation, the Project aimed to take Bigfoot tracking to new levels by uncovering where the creatures shelter and nest between observations. Their patience paid off tremendously when the team stumbled upon a series of intriguing structures bearing remarkable hallmarks of being constructed by massive primates.

The Olympic Project founding members included Derek Randles, David Ellis, and Cameron Gosse together with consultant Shane Corson who worked closely with the U.S. Forest Service. The team specialized in systematic grid searches employing game cameras, sound recordings, footprint casting, and nest profiling techniques refined over years in the field. Their discovery of mysterious nest-like structures constructed high in tree canopies provided rare glimpses into how these creatures might reside in the dense Pacific Northwest forests long described by Native tribes as home to the "hairy giants of the woods."

In July 2013, while investigating promising areas pinpointed by a heat-signature drone survey, the team noticed several bizarre constructions hidden amongst thick tree branches dozens of feet above ground. Using zoom lenses and binoculars, they observed details suggesting these served as shelters or nests rather than natural debris piles accumulated through storms. The distinctly bowl-shaped structures incorporated woven tree boughs lined with grasses, ferns, and moss all bent and twisted together into cohesive units sturdy enough for holding considerable weight.

Team members estimated dimensions reached 5-6 feet across and 3 feet high - exponentially larger than any nests built by known local wildlife. The scale, composition materials, and placement so high in trees pointed to builders with big brains and bodies to match. Studying the scene, the Project founders couldn't help but share a stunned collective realization. Every visible detail perfectly matched expectations for shelter-building handiwork of Sasquatch-type creatures reported roaming the region for generations.

The structures clearly supported the idea that large primates had bent, broke, and intertwined living woody branches into shape. The team noted how branches remained green with no signs of snapping from weakness or rot. Moss and forest debris formed a sturdy bowl-shape able to hold over 1,000 pounds if built by creatures reported to reach 10 feet and weigh up to 500 pounds or more. And positioning dozens of feet high in the canopy fit perfectly with theories of how such tall, powerful beasts might securely rest off the ground.

When consulting primate specialists, the researchers learned such nest-building methods aligned remarkably with gorillas, chimpanzees, and other forest apes known to construct tree-bound sleeping platforms high in the canopy. Researchers expressed fascination that no known species in North America exhibited this behavior. The only logical explanation seemed attribution to undocumented New World apes with instincts for weaving sturdy arboreal shelters.

The Olympic Project immediately intensified exploration in the discovery zone searching for further signs of Bigfoot habitation. Just two miles away, the team located another series of nest-like structures in a tightly concentrated area suggesting a preferred shelter hot spot. One particularly large construct measured over 8 feet across - enough to accommodate a very substantial primate frame. Trail cameras monitoring the location yielded 14,000 images but none displayed the elusive builders in action. However, the search perimeter did reveal intriguing giant footprints in mud and multiple intriguing hair tufts caught on branches.

DNA analysis later matched some hair samples to known wildlife but others yielded confusing results with anomalous primate markers suggesting possible Bigfoot origin. Unfortunately, poor DNA preservation from the elements prohibited conclusive species identification. Still, combined with the compelling nest discovery, the Olympic Project team felt confident announcing to media that significant new evidence supported theories of an undocumented North American ape inhabiting remote Pacific Northwest rainforests.

Mainstream scientists scoffed at this extraordinary claim by Bigfoot devotees long considered a fringe element in cryptozoology circles. Primatologists outside of zoos consulted for initial nest site reactions argued no definitive conclusions could be drawn without more exhaustive evaluation ruling out all other options first. But they did agree no known species satisfactorily explained the nest structures' immense scale and composition. The discovery raised perplexing questions about what exactly might have constructed these elaborate woody shelters.

The Project founders anticipated resistance from closed-minded academics but pushed forward with additional field work to build their case. Over 150 miles away in a remote area of southern Washington, they uncovered another series of nest-like formations in the canopy of old growth forest. Once again, the scale and intricacy suggested massive primates weaving living tree limbs into platforms holding hundreds of pounds. This consistent evidence hundreds of miles apart strengthened the team's conviction that an unknown population of hominins inhabited the region rather than one-off anomalies.

Critics dismissed these claims by highlighting that no Bigfoot specimen or body has ever surfaced to validate existence of such giants. Mainstream biology rejects suggesting an unknown higher primate related to humans could inhabit North America without prior documentation. But Project members pointed to many species discoveries beginning with limited evidence like these nests before more conclusive proof comes later. Circumstantial data still carries weight when consistent patterns defy simpler explanations.

They explained how many new megafauna species identifications start with indigenous people guiding researchers to areas displaying signs of something anomalous. Intriguing evidence accumulates until science can no longer ignore the burgeoning probability of a new species avoiding detection. The nest discovery signaled reaching that tipping point for acknowledging a rare North American ape.

While lacking a type specimen or definitive video footage, the Olympic Project researchers emphasized that proof encompasses a mosaic of evidence building undeniable weight over time. Consistently documented behaviors like nest-building point to underlying biology behind fleeting sightings even if direct genetic evidence remains elusive. No species inhabits a region for centuries without leaving behind signs of sheltering behaviors.

Discoveries like massive nests constructed high in forest canopies provide those critical behavioral clues that can guide future identification efforts by highlighting where to focus search areas and trail camera monitoring. Rather than chasing footprints aimlessly, the Olympic Project leveraged local habitat clues to zero in on promising hot spots more strategically. Their success finding intriguing evidence in concentrated zones validated this habitat-centric strategy.

The nest structures also supply additional context for interpreting longstanding Native accounts of these forest giants. Indigenous stories depict behaviors like intricate nest construction passed down across generations - subtle details that lend authenticity through accurate environmental alignments with direct field observations. This nest discovery powerfully connected modern evidence with ancient oral traditions supporting the reality of giant hairy forest dwellers in the region.

While the Olympic Project team recognizes much work remains to convince conservative scientists, they believe continuing field work centered around forest habitats will ultimately provide the proof needed. As detection technologies like drones and remote sensing cameras improve, tracking these elusive creatures back to nesting sites and shelter hot spots offers the best opportunity to finally document their existence.

Patience and an open mind to seemingly inexplicable evidence leads to revelations about nature's outstanding mysteries. Rather than quick dismissal of such extraordinary finds, science must allow the evidence to accumulate until the reality of an undocumented species becomes undeniable. The nest discovery highlighted that seeking signs of habitation provides a powerful lens for focusing that gradual proof-building process.

The Olympic Project's pioneering work demonstrated that strategic searches of remote wildlands can uncover tangible artifacts of Bigfoot existence even if direct encounters remain unlikely. Their success locating intriguing ground nests and immense aerial platforms made from intricately woven tree limbs offers templates for other research groups to follow in the quest to prove these giants exist. Such consistent evidence of elaborate shelters built high in forest canopies points to one inevitable conclusion - something with keen engineering instincts has made North America's remote mountain forests its home, awaiting final acknowledgment that it's more than mere legend.

Deciphering Bigfoot's Tree Knocking Code

In remote forests from Washington to Florida, campers and hikers have reported hearing loud, unexplained knocking sounds echoing through the woods. The percussive bangs, said to mimic the pattern of human knocking on a front door, often occur in sets of three spaced several seconds apart. In many cases the witnesses can find no rational source for these jarring raps against hard surfaces like tree trunks or rock walls. Over decades of accounts, the legend has arisen that this cryptic code is a form of communication used by Bigfoot.

What could cause these enigmatic sounds? If legitimate, what meaning may lie behind the tree and rock knocks in their various observed patterns? Could it really be the work of a Sasquatch, and if so what are they trying to convey? In this chapter we will analyze this phenomenon deeply: the history of encounters, scientific theories behind the sounds, patterns and meanings that may constitute a language, and how it fits into the search for conclusive proof.

History and Notable Incidents

While rock clacking and wood knocking have occurred in folklore and Native American legends for centuries, detailed documentation began in the late 1960s as the concept of an undiscovered North American ape gained traction in the public imagination. Certain areas of high concentration of knocks have emerged over the decades:

- The Appalachians of rural Pennsylvania, West Virginia and North Carolina, where loud knocks have accompanied many visual sightings.
- The Sierra Nevada mountains of California, where the wildlands provide ample hiding space.
- The swamps and forests of Florida, where the climate could support a small population.

- The Pacific Northwest, encompassing the forests of northern California through British Columbia, where the most famous case originated.

In 1982, late at night in a rural area outside Seattle, a property owner investigated strange sounds and sighted a large hair-covered creature outside his home. When he attempted to pursue with a flashlight, he was met with a series of high-pitched screams and three distinct knocks on the cedar walls of his house. The incident was covered in the news and spawned widespread interest in the knocks potentially being a Bigfoot signal.

Explanations Behind the Sounds

Several rational explanations have been proposed: falling branches striking trees or debris piles, rockslides in mountain forests, expanding ice or earth movements in colder climates, or even pranksters armed with baseball bats. But most lack consistency with the described incidents: precise patterns to the knocks, vast remoteness of many locations, and incidents accompanied by visual sightings and footprints.

If indeed made by Bigfoot knuckles or tools, what physical traits allow them to produce such loud percussions? Analysis shows a one inch thick cedar board could be struck without fracture at a velocity of 25 miles per hour by a fist approximately ten inches wide. An eight-foot-tall Sasquatch weighing 800 pounds could easily achieve knocking energy several times greater than a human. Long arms adding leverage, thick palm bones layered for protection, and incredible musculature explain feats like shaking sturdy campers or throwing 400-pound rocks. In short, a Bigfoot could produce knocks of deafening amplitude.

As for how more rapid knock sequences are produced, the most plausible explanation is that two hands are used alternately to generate the signature 1-2-3 beat associated with wood knocks.

What Could the Knocks Mean?

Deciphering a potential language depends on studying the observed patterns and hypothesizing meaning. Reports describe several variations:

- Single knocks at irregular intervals, as if from roaming individuals
- Groups of 2-3 knocks made in rapid succession, then silence for up to 20 seconds
- Sequential groups sounding over several minutes, moving steadily across a ridge or valley
- Exchanges of multiple groups back and forth, avoiding direct interaction

Linguistic experts surmise this shows an intended communication much more complex than just signaling a location. Single knocks may simply allow wandering members of a group to identify positions after separation, or signal a desire to regroup. Sets of double or triple knocks could share richer meanings - communicating danger, claiming territory, or requesting a meeting. Extended exchanges may relate to conflict mediation, coordination of migration to seasonal feeding areas, or even mating overtures.

In other words, a rudimentary form of language likely used within family clusters or the larger collective of a Bigfoot tribe. Perhaps these signals developed not only as practical tools but also cultural traditions allowing communities to thrive undetected for centuries.

Frustratingly, beyond tantalizing clues, the sparse data makes deciphering concrete meaning difficult. And therein lies the dilemma for cryptozoologists seeking answers through habituation: any attempt to replicate knock patterns risks scaring off these elusive creatures. Like dolphin signature whistles or whale song, to truly decode the language may require years of patient listening.

How Knocks Fit into Future Discoveries

For serious Bigfoot researchers, authenticating wood knocks as a form of Sasquatch communication could provide an invaluable tool in proving their existence. If sound recordings could definitively link knock patterns to visual sightings and footprint discoveries in a predictive way, it would enable more reliable tracking of their migration routes, preferred habitats, and population densities in a given region.

In that sense, potentially developing a Bigfoot call dictionary could be as useful for conservation efforts as teaching gorillas sign language has been. Of course, most zoological fields rely heavily on scat, hair and blood samples for study before recognizing new species. So while knocks offer promise for study, the holy grail remains DNA evidence, such as hair follicles snagged on tree bark confirming the origin of these signals.

In the end, wood knocks represent just one small facet of the Bigfoot legend - albeit an eerie one for those hearing unexplained forest sounds at night. They join the accumulated decades of plaster casts, intriguing videos, and consistent eyewitness reports to strengthen the argument that an undiscovered North American ape walks among us. Perhaps in time, patient science and emerging technologies will help us reliably translate the true meaning behind these cryptic messages echoing through the darkness. For those seeking answers, the knocking signals hope.

The Controversial Science of Sasquatch Scat

Among the various forms of proof a cryptid like Bigfoot might leave behind, the least glamorous and most controversial is scat - the scientific term for animal feces. Yet consistent discoveries of anomalous fecal samples in remote forests have sparked debate within the cryptozoology community. Could these enigmatic droppings provide the smoking gun to prove a small population of relic hominids roams North America?

In this chapter, we objectively examine this taboo line of evidence: the history of samples uncovered, scientific analysis performed, issues facing validation, and how scat ultimately factors into the hunt for hidden creatures like Sasquatch.

Early Samples and Field Research

Reports of unusual manure or waste date back decades in areas of alleged Bigfoot activity. The earliest serious study began in the 1960s with Ivan Sanderson, who developed strict protocols for discovering and documenting rare animal scat. Sanderson cataloged over 200 abnormal droppings across eastern states he believed could have originated from an unknown primate.

In 1982, biologist John Bindernagel found sizeable dung piles in remote British Columbia containing strange twisted pieces of plant matter that matched nothing from recognized wildlife. Respected primatologist John Napier studied the Bindernagel samples and commented that while far from conclusive, they shared similarities to great ape feces and warranted further analysis.

The most rigorous field work occurred in the 1990s under renowned primate authority Dr. Jeff Meldrum. His expeditions uncovered dozens of specimens he considered anomalous, notably in the Blue Mountains region of southeastern Washington state. Meldrum's strict collection methodology ruled out contamination and ensured rapid laboratory analysis.

Common Traits and Challenges

The notable samples share some recurring characteristics, while also presenting scientific obstacles:

- Sizeable volume - over a quart in many cases, far exceeding human or black bear amounts
- Consistency - solid and cohesive with visible plant matter rather than loose or liquid
- Odor - often described as pungent, nauseating or akin to rotting meat
- Remoteness - found deep in vast wilderness, ruling out livestock or most wildlife
- No tracks/signs - lack of footprints/trails indicates upright posture
- Temperature - samples rarely warm, precluding conclusive DNA testing
- Weathering - rapid decomposition in damp climates like the Pacific Northwest
- No established baseline - no prior Sasquatch scat for comparison

The lack of other contextual evidence (tracks, hair, etc.) and rapid decay causing samples to degrade before lab testing can commence have stymied efforts to present scat as compelling proof for Bigfoot believers. Still, experts argue the volume and composition point to a large omnivorous primate.

DNA Challenges and Successes

Isolating intact DNA has proven enormously difficult from Bigfoot scat, which skeptics claim is simply the expected result from wild animals. The reality is somewhat more complex.

Fecal matter, by nature, contains fragmented biological material making DNA matching a challenge. Water, heat and bacteria rapidly break down cellular structures. Yet even deer and elk droppings yield identifiable genetics when fresh.

The problem is we have no established Bigfoot genetic baseline for comparison, leaving researchers stuck in a catch-22. Thus DNA analysis has been limited to excluding known species and searching for anomalies. One result yielded mitochondrial DNA suggesting a relation to humans but not matching any known primate. Unfortunately later tests were inconclusive, and the sample eventually became too degraded to retest.

Frustratingly, this exemplifies both the potential and pitfalls of scat research. Genetic tools require intact, pure samples collected and preserved rapidly under controlled conditions prior to sequencing. Field conditions rarely allow this, causing the window of opportunity for viable DNA matching to quickly close.

Still, new gene sequencing technology offers hope, and if more verifiable samples were discovered, a genetic catalog of regional Sasquatch variations might eventually form. In that quest, scat could provide the same clues hair and blood do for other species.

How Scat Advances the Search

For serious Bigfoot scientists, proving a clear link between unusual scat samples and the creature's existence remains a "gold standard" for evidence. Conclusively matching genetics or biochemical traits between fresh samples and independtly verified visual sightings or footprint casts would cement the reality of Sasquatch. In that respect, manure offers easier collection than hair or blood.

The other advantage of reputable scat discoveries is focusing search areas and patterns. If samples created identifiable regional profiles, migration routes and population densities could be tracked like other endangered species.

Of course, feces will always lack the emotional impact of an HD video or captured specimen. And "squatch poop" jokes will surely persist in pop culture. But all science begins with observations, and patterns among those observations. In that sense, the persistent discovery of anomalous scat keeps alive the possibility of a shy, unrecognized North American primate. One that science may yet conclusively show itself to, by learning from what it leaves behind.

Reading the Signs of Sasquatch in the Wilderness

In the remote forests of the Pacific Northwest, alert hikers occasionally stumble upon mysterious signs suggesting they are not alone. Felled trees twisted unnaturally, massive boulder fields clearly disturbed, or peculiar constructions of wood and rock that seem almost ceremonial in purpose. Sites like these form another category in the circumstantial case for Bigfoot's existence - through telltale impact on their environment.

What clues might these trace remnants of activity provide? Could the cause be ordinary but the interpretation skewed by legend? Or might these markers in the deep wilderness betray the presence of a rare intelligent beast remarkably adept at leaving few traces? In this chapter we examine documented cases, common traits, challenges to confirmation, and how this ephemeral evidence factors into the enigma of North America's "great hairy man" of the woods.

Key Discoveries Over the Years

Sporadic accounts of odd environmental traces possibly attributable to Bigfoot go back over a century in local indigenous lore, pioneer journals, and newspaper records. But wider awareness grew in 1958 when road construction crews in Northern California discovered gigantic humanoid footprints alongside disturbed machinery one morning. The credibility of heavy equipment operators spurred public imagination despite an absence of sightings.

In the 1960s, strange occurrences surfaced in the Palouse prairies of eastern Washington where gigantic trampled grass beds, dubbed "Sasquatch nests", suggested huge creatures bedding down in remote fields. Zoologists judged the patterns and flattened vegetation inconsistent with livestock or known wildlife. Locals believed the nests indicated seasonal migration habits.

A milestone event came in 1994 near Mt. St. Helens when a retired U.S. Forest Service employee discovered an area of hillside where entire mature trees had been twisted, stripped and arranged in patterns seemingly to create shelter formations. The former timber professional could find no natural explanation for the complex formations. The site was exhaustively documented and remains one of the most extensive environmental trace cases.

Common Themes and Characteristics

Examining key locations reveals recurring profile markers:

- Damage requiring extreme strength – thick pine trees snapped midway up, large boulders clearly displaced
- Seemingly purposeful arrangements – pine bough beds shaped for reclining, log shelters with views of valleys
- Twisted, not chopped damage – tree branches wrung loose leaving fibers stretched not cut
- Selective foraging signs – certain plants uprooted, berries stripped, ant hills raided
- No foot trails in/out – implying origins able to climb/descend steep slopes easily
- Terrain inaccessible to vehicles – ruling out human origins

While any one case alone leaves doubts, together the patterns defy straightforward attribution to known natural or human activity. And while proof remains lacking, the commonalities suggest a large, intelligent forager occupying remote sanctuaries.

Challenges to Confirming Origins

The ephemeral nature of these fleeting signs of disturbance inevitably raises skepticism rather than acceptance in the overly rational. Without direct evidence like camera footage, collecting hair or scat samples for DNA matching, or even tracks or smells, many dismiss the sites as misinterpreted.

The sheer remoteness of locations means few qualified experts reach them before weathering obscures clues. Photos or soil imprints alone rarely suffice to sway scientific consensus. Preserving crime scene-like trace evidence protocols is near impossible in dense wilderness. And hoaxing remains a concern, especially post-publicity.

Yet proponents argue these persistent "hot spots" share genuine traits that stretch coincidence. What rational explanations might account for the documented sites?

Evaluating and Debunking Common Counter-Explanations:

- Bear activity – Black bears lack the size and dexterity to apply leverage tools or construct shelters. Grizzlies are not indigenous to the Pacific coast.
- Bigfoot hunters – No vehicle access to remote trail-less terrain. Areas lack human refuse or camouflage materials.
- Property developers – Pristine locations lack utility access. Site arrangements have no commercial purpose.
- Storm/seismic damage – Selective breakage patterns not consistent with winds or quakes. Stable weather documented.
- Forest canopy damage – No visible canopy gaps from falling trees. Trunks remain rooted.

While no theory fully addresses the facts, the great ape hypothesis aligns most closely.

How Environmental Traces Support Bigfoot's Case

These ephemeral signs of activity, while rarely standalone proof, still strengthen the cumulative argument for Sasquatch's reality. They demonstrate the biggest empirical gap in the species' survival prospects:

A sustainable breeding population would require steady access to abundant food sources across western wildlands. Reports of selective foraging do illustrate specialized knowledge of edible vegetation. And a migratory range spanning California to Canada is ecologically feasible.

Additionally, shelter building and nest construction suggest higher intelligence and tool use. While gorillas and chimpanzees craft rudimentary sleeping platforms in trees and brush, structuring pine boughs into weatherproof refuge implies more advanced reasoning.

So while scattered damage brings Bigfoot no closer to recognized species status, the patterns lend credence to First Nations oral traditions. Undiscovered populations leave their mark on the land when we know how to spot the signs. The undiscovered may only remain so until we open our senses to perceive them.

Reading the Outlines Left Behind in Remote Wilderness

In isolated meadows and remote forest clearings, hikers occasionally encounter odd shapes and depressions in vegetation and soil lacking any obvious cause. Some discover outlines of large bodies seemingly pressed into grass or imprinted on the ground. Others find bowl-like nests trampled from thick brush. A few even report strange piles of ferns or leaves apparently gathered then abandoned. While any single instance easily dismisses as questionable, together they form a pattern - of size, geography and behavior consistent with theories of an elusive great ape inhabiting the Pacific Northwest.

In this chapter we examine the history and common traits around these obscure anomalies found across the wilderness, evaluate explanations for their origins, and consider how they bolster the argument for lingering North American populations of large primate species like Gigantopithecus surviving undocumented in the deep forests.

Early Discoveries and Hotspot Regions

As with Bigfoot evidence broadly, Native American oral traditions contain references to large, wild "forest people" leaving signs of their passing in remote areas. But recorded documentation traces back to pioneer settlers and early 20th century loggers reporting finding gigantic sleeping hollows after forest fires consumed brush. The earliest known body print dates to 1924 when berry pickers near Mt. St. Helens in southern Washington state found 13-inch depressions sunk four inches into soil in a marshy meadow.

In the 1950s and 60s multiple instances of very large body impressions - some over seven feet long - and crushed areas of vegetation appeared in rural regions of Washington, Oregon and British Columbia. And a strange pattern of discovery sites situated on the outskirts of small isolated towns dotted the map. While any single small town report proved questionable, together the geography and timing suggested a migratory creature periodically encroaching on civilization then retreating.

Key Characteristics and Theories

Common traits emerge in the most credible reports:

- Length over 5 feet - ruling out known wildlife
- Depth several inches - requiring substantial weight
- Outline of head, arms and legs - consistent with hominid shape
- Located sizeable distances into forests - no vehicle access
- Discovered near seasonal food sources - berries, fish runs, etc.

And while any individual site leaves ample doubt, scientific analysis of depth, shape and soil disruption make random causes unlikely across so many impressions. In particular, the discovery of 14" long foot shapes accompanying body forms links them circumstantially to Bigfoot evidence categories like tracks and nest constructions.

If indeed made by undocumented creatures, what explanations fit?

The impressions tend to locate in areas offering shelter and seasonal food useful to large omnivores. This implies purposeful movement and diet. The outline shapes indicate resting postures - not random falling. And the weight needed to compress soil and vegetation shows enough bulk to exclude known species. Altogether the signs point to stealthy giants roaming forests.

Challenges to Confirming Origins

Like all Bigfoot trace evidence not linked to direct sightings, photos or tissue samples, the ephemeral body marks offer no testable proof of origins - only clues subject to interpretation.

With no viable organic matter left behind, dating techniques like carbon 14 analysis remain impossible. And no chemical composition or DNA testing can confirm if a given impression originated from a man, beast or questionable source. Locations hundreds of miles apart and separated by decades essentially rely on eyewitness credibility, limits of photo evidence, and faith in forensic shape analysis.

The lack of falsifiable evidence leaves the door open for counter explanations:

- Hoaxers using body molds to create shapes
- Bear rolls flattening vegetation
- Groups camping illegally deep in remote areas
- ATV riders trespassing across public lands
- Property developers surveying sites illegally

With no means to conclusively disprove these alternative theories, body impressions remain "evidence of absence" rather than proof of existence.

How They Support the Sasquatch Argument

While the evidence category perhaps offers less value than Bigfoot videos or DNA samples, the odd body impressions still advance the argument for acceptance of Sasquatch in key ways:

First, they display consistent anatomical profiles - arms, legs, head and shoulders pressed into soil rather than random oval depressions. This implies a creature not only able but choosing to lay prone to rest, eat or observe.

Second, the discovery geography correlates to other evidence traces like nests, food gathering signs, tree and rock manipulations. This strengthens the case for a migratory species following seasonal food sources and shelter needs.

Third, the outlines found to date, whether all legitimate or not, still demonstrate ongoing public intrigue and desire to believe in the creature's reality. As with less validated evidence forms like eyewitness reports, they reveal the depth of cultural legend.

Finally, imprints left behind, even faint and questionable ones, reflect the analogy of absence as presence. Much like astronomers inferring planets orbiting distant stars by gravitational ripples too faint to observe directly, the intermittent body outlines across untamed American wilderness hint at lifeforms leaving their ephemeral mark in the remote darkness. Life that intends to remain unseen but fails by slight degrees. And while too tenuous alone to declare new species, the overlooked impressions cataloged together call to the open-minded from the silence.

Does an unknown giant slumber in North America's unexplored forests? The impressions suggest more research needed to find out.

The Tantalizing Quest for Sasquatch Genetic Proof

In the scientific realm, the gold standard for documenting a new species rests on DNA analysis - unlocking the genomic code held within tissue, hair, blood or scat samples. This branch of Bigfoot evidence has long tantalized cryptozoologists. If indisputable DNA could link samples to an unknown primate, skepticism would transform to confirmed discovery. Yet the few tests conducted over the decades have remained ambiguous or disputed as contaminated or hoaxes. What light have the results to date shed? How close have researchers come to definitive evidence? And what obstacles exist to proving a genetic basis for Bigfoot's reality?

History of Testing Efforts

In the early 1990s, interest arose around recovering DNA from unusual hair and scat samples discovered in wilderness areas spanning the Pacific Northwest region down to the Southern U.S. Several university labs conducted DNA amplification tests seeking identifiable genetic markers. But the analysis only yielded non-specific results attributed to known local wildlife, or contaminated samples lacking controls to eliminate doubts.

Through the 2000s, better collection practices emerged but technology and high costs still limited findings. Most test results traced back to black bears, wolves or even cattle roaming national forests from illegal grazing. However in 2013, a European lab did sequence mitochondrial DNA from a sample found in the Olympic Peninsula suggesting human ancestry but with enough anomalies to exclude known apes or tribal genetics. Unfortunately the small fragments degraded before nuclear DNA could undergo extraction and genome mapping for positive identification.

By 2020, rapid advances in genetic testing created new optimism around conclusively linking samples to Bigfoot origin. But when Texas officials had several hair and blood samples analyzed after reported sightings, the DNA matched local deer and raccoon profiles. The latest Florida report from 2021 followed suit, identifying black bear and feral hog markers, deflating another claim.

Barriers to Obtaining Testable Samples

The failure to generate verifiable, testable DNA evidence over decades of searching highlights the immense difficulties in procuring and studying biological material from rare and elusive species. Several factors impede Bigfoot in particular:

- Sparse numbers across vast wild areas lessens odds of encounters with tissue left behind
- Field conditions rapidly degrade organic matter before proper retrieval
- Lack of an established genetic baseline sample of Sasquatch DNA against which to compare
- No captive specimen to provide control DNA
- Risk of hoaxing and contamination absent rigorous collection protocols

The reality is that without a baseline profile to reference, even clear DNA results linking to an unknown primate would face doubts given histories of hoaxes muddying public perception.

Promising Paths Forward

Still, DNA holds unique potential for definitively documenting new species, even extremely rare ones. Emerging technical advances offer hope for overcoming past barriers:

- Portable field DNA sequencers could allow results from fresh samples in remote sites
- Digital genomic database comparisons against all cataloged land mammals
- Algorithmic analysis to detect genetic chimera indicators of undiscovered hybrid species

- Dedicated sample testing facilities adhering to forensic collection protocols

Cryptozoologists remain confident that obtaining multiple DNA sample matches across geography and decades would establish legitimacy even absent an initial control. Like all great discoveries, it may require patience combined with faith in science.

And if Bigfoot originated as a remnant of Gigantopithecus, an offshoot branch of early humans, or even a new subspecies, its genetic heritage surely leaves clues waiting to be decoded. Skeptics consider the species a legend sustained by wishful thinking. But legends permeate cultures for reasons. And one irrefutable DNA match could transform legend into zoological reality. For a creature so adept at avoiding cameras and capture, genetics may offer the only path to draw the reclusive hominid fully into the light at last.

While the accumulated eyewitness accounts, videos, and environmental traces such as nests and trackways build a compelling circumstantial case, the lack of a type specimen or DNA evidence still hampers definitive scientific confirmation of Bigfoot's existence. But from the 1960s onward as public fascination grew, dedicated amateur groups began organizing more formally across North America to document sightings, study habitats, and search for physical evidence in the remote forests where encounters occur.

In the next chapter we profile some of the most prominent Bigfoot research organizations that emerged over the past 50 years. Staffed by passionate volunteer teams alongside credentialed scientists lending their expertise, these groups represent the vanguard compiling sighting reports, interviewing witnesses, and mounting expeditions to remote areas seeking irrefutable proof. We explore their history, methods, use of technology, and views on why conclusive evidence remains so elusive. Their perspectives from the front lines of the hunt reveal what still prevents the legendary beast from finally stepping out of the shadows into the spotlight at last.

Bigfoot research teams

Inside BFRO: The World's Leading Bigfoot Hunting Organization

Founded in 1995, the Bigfoot Field Researchers Organization, or BFRO, has grown into the most prominent and active group investigating sightings and searching for conclusive evidence to prove the creature's existence. Their expansive database of reports spanning the continent reveals persistent encounters happening more frequently than commonly believed. But despite amassing intriguing trace evidence, capturing definitive proof has proven enormously challenging.

In this chapter, we explore BFRO's origins, field site investigations, use of technology, organization of expeditions, and perspective on why Sasquatch continues evading cameras and scientists after all these years.

History and Approach

The BFRO emerged from discussions in internet forums populated by individuals sharing personal Bigfoot sighting accounts when few mainstream outlets took such stories seriously. Members began systematically documenting detailed reports behind the scenes using investigative protocols. By the mid 90s they launched a public website that quickly began accumulating hundreds more accounts to their database that approached ten thousand reports by 2022.

Despite sensational public perceptions of Bigfoot believers, BFRO membership consists primarily of serious outdoor enthusiasts well familiar with wildlife. Their investigative approach collects witness interviews, revisits sites to search for physical traces, deploys remote trail cameras in hot spots and leverages technologies like thermal imaging to systematically scour remote terrain. They convene annual conferences discussing collected evidence and recent studies.

While lacking direct university affiliations to allow access to certain tools like genetics labs, BFRO collaborates respected primatologists, anthropologists and wildlife officials as much as possible bringing scientific rigor. Their position straddles a line between grassroots amateur investigation and professional field work.

Expeditions and Technology Use

A core BFRO initiative involves organizing field expeditions where members can explore prime habitat areas and investigate recent sighting locations more thoroughly in teams.

These multi-day forays convene seasoned researchers leading small groups new to investigating for immersive educational experiences about Bigfoot ecology. Hikes survey terrain while nights see deployment of thermography, seismic sensors and amplified audio gear to detect activity under cover of darkness. Advanced drone and remote camera traps monitor valley corridors hoping to snare the elusive giants on film.

To date dozens of expeditions have uncovered tantalizing evidence - from nests and track casts to tree structures and strange vocal recordings. But no singular smoking gun sighting or DNA confirmation has yet occurred. Still, the field work allows systematic testing of the latest surveillance technologies within the enormous challenge of monitoring millions of wilderness acres, mostly in roadless areas.

Why No Definitive Proof Yet?

After decades collecting reports and mounting expeditions, the lack of irrefutable evidence inevitably frustrates the BFRO and similar organizations. Their position hardens against dismissals that the legendary giants are imaginary or extinct. Thousands of eyewitnesses spanning generations cannot all be delusional. Too many reputable professionals with wildlife expertise contribute accounts. And the volume reaches 10+ incidents reported a day across North America in recent years - far more than publicly assumed.

So why does definitive proof remain so elusive? The BFRO points to key factors:

- Small overall populations likely number a few thousand at most across an immense landscape spanning the Pacific Northwest to the Eastern woodlands - a tiny density making chance encounters extremely rare.
- Their nocturnal nature means most activity occurs under cover of darkness when visibility proves extremely challenging.
- As intelligent, social creatures they have developed expert avoidance behaviors to maximize secrecy, especially wary of humans.
- The climate and dense vegetation accelerate decomposition, minimizing fossils or recent remains surfacing before scavenging.

Yet the group remains confident the odds of capturing conclusive evidence mount steadily as remote camera sensor capabilities expand alongside DNA technologies. In their view, obtaining irrefutable proof of Bigfoot's reality remains not an "if" but a "when" in the near future. Perhaps one of their upcoming expeditions will finally cement the giant hominid's rightful place in the annals of documented species, reveling a new chapter for biology from the ancient forests.

The North American Wood Ape Conservancy

Seeking Proof and Protection

Founded in 2002, the North American Wood Ape Conservancy (NAWAC) constitutes one of the only non-profit groups dedicated specifically to researching and protecting the cryptid hominid if substantiated as an extant species. Their name for Bigfoot - the "Wood Ape" - conveys this conservation ethos further, eschewing sensational pop culture terms to emphasize scientific documentation and habitat stewardship.

In this chapter we explore NAWAC's unique origins, field work methodology, use of technology, perspective on why conclusive evidence remains elusive, and how they would shift to formal species protection efforts if granted the evidence needed to sway science.

History and Approach

NAWAC emerged from discussions between primate researchers and conservationists who grew intrigued by the persistent flow of alleged Bigfoot sightings originating from many trained biologists, foresters and wildlife officials themselves across certain southern states. This lent more credibility to the possibility of an undocumented ape inhabiting North American forests.

They began operating small research teams to establish baseline population numbers should the creature prove reality. Field work emphasizes scouring remote wildlands for evidence, deploying camera traps, and collecting biological samples for genetics analysis. In recent years, the group has focused intently on areas of Oklahoma and Texas where frequent recent sightings occur near the endangered Red Wolf recovery zone.

NAWAC collaborates respectfully with indigenous First Nations bands in research areas, acknowledging their oral traditions were first to reference the "tall men of the woods" known locally as the Chiye Tankah. They also work closely with wildlife officials in case protected species legislation becomes warranted.

While much of NAWAC's preliminary activity mirrors other amateur Bigfoot investigator groups, their niche emphasis on conservation ecology and genetics analysis takes a longer view - to scientifically prove the species exists as a prerequisite to ever protecting its future.

Field Work and Technology Use

NAWAC deploys field teams to remote forest regions where recent credible sightings have surfaced, especially near the Red Wolf range. Ground surveys search for tracks, nests, and other physical evidence. Perimeter camera traps monitor for images night and day, while mobile thermal scopes scan valley corridors.

To avoid contamination, stringent collection protocols govern any hair, scat or nest materials to allow university genetics labs to sequence DNA for anomalies. Soil impression casts get scanned for archiving and analysis by primate experts. Audio recordings capture sounds for expert evaluation. Photogrammetry recreates print contours and dermal ridges in 3D models.

In essence, NAWAC field work emphasizes scientific precision aligned to species verification and habitat conservation goals rather than recreational hobbyists seeking their own sighting trophy. Still, definitive proof remains forthcoming.

Why No Definitive Proof Yet?

While adopting state-of-the-art tools in the search, NAWAC's perspective on the lack of scientific confirmation mirrors all groups spending decades analyzing the mystery - the creatures display intelligence on par with the great apes combined with innate wariness toward humans and human technology. They have also honed concealment abilities over eons to exploit their remote forest niches. Only by mastering their avoidance techniques can man hope to finally document their existence.

NAWAC notes the many obstacles: dense canopy and vegetation, scarce traces, small widely dispersed populations, overnight erosion of tracks, and the vastness of undeveloped land preventing grid sweeps. Thermal signatures prove indistinguishable from other large mammals. And expeditions risk permanently scaring them off if not conducted cautiously. The margin for error spans razor thin for capturing the necessary proof before the creatures vanish into deeper isolation.

Preparing for Protection

Still, NAWAC remains dedicated to the premise that even robust evidence short of a body will eventually precipitate policy shifts. Once scientific consensus passes a certain threshold of probability, the "wood apes" will qualify as an endangered species.

Only then would formal habitat protections, population monitoring, anti-poaching deterrence and other conservation mechanisms engage. For a shy beast long adapted to avoiding humanity, this poses an ironic outcome - forced to trust people in order to save it from people. But NAWAC stands poised to marshal that future effort once the proof surfaces to pull Sasquatch fully into the light at last. Where it goes next remains wild as the forests it emerges from.

The Sasquatch Genome Project Controversy

In genetics science, few milestones would rival sequencing DNA conclusively proving an unknown hominid species inhabits North America alongside modern humans. But extraordinary claims require extraordinary evidence to overcome skepticism. And few Bigfoot cases challenge credibility like the bombshell press release issued in 2013 by Dr. Melba Ketchum, a Texas veterinarian and genetics businessman.

Ketchum founded the Sasquatch Genome Project in 2010 aiming to document definitive genetic proof by collecting and analyzing biological samples obtained by other researchers around North America. After three years of secrecy, her team announced completion of the "first study of its kind to scientifically address the formal identification of the species commonly known as Bigfoot." Their shocking claim: the evidence suggests an unknown human-hybrid cross thousands of years ago between female Homo sapiens and male ancestors of modern apes or extinct hominids like Gigantopithecus.

In this chapter we review the purported Ketchum DNA study, the reaction of the scientific establishment, and the lingering controversy over whether the findings constitute profound discovery or unproven pseudoscience.

A Blockbuster Announcement

In a widely covered February 2013 press release, Ketchum announced DNA sequencing of 111 specimens - blood, tissue, hair, and other items forwarded to her lab by Bigfoot enthusiasts and field researchers over several years. The samples allegedly originated from various wilderness areas across the U.S. Her report described rigorous forensic protocols to prevent contamination and ensure sample purity.

Using forensic genomics tools tailored to detect even fragmented DNA, her team detailed electron microscope imagery of new microscopic structures discovered in the blood as well as sequencing indicating triple DNA strands never observed before - ostensibly proving a "new mammalian hybrid species" in North America they dubbed "Homo Sapiens Cognatus". Ketchum asserted this directly challenged the current scientific consensus on evolution and required reconsideration of accepted human ancestry.

Fierce Criticisms Emerge

Despite substantial media coverage, the provocative Bigfoot DNA claims met swift condemnation from the scientific establishment regarding credibility of the group's research integrity and methodology.

Critics assailed the lack of reputable genetics lab corroboration, absence of external peer-review before self-publishing results, failure to provide raw data for verification, questionable journal selection for publication, and inability of others to replicate unique DNA findings for validation. Some even implied deliberate data manipulation was likely from a lab without accreditation.

Until rigorous independent replication occurs, most academics dismiss the Ketchum DNA claims as falling well short of scientific proof. Others argue that without a type specimen, definitive genetic evidence proving Bigfoot remains essentially impossible.

A Stain on Cryptozoology?

For a field seeking credibility before conservative science, the Ketchum DNA episode proved a sizable setback. Even sympathetic supporters cringed at her media blitz overpromising before establishing consensus around such extraordinary assertions. The botched peer-review and slapdash publication reinforced stereotypes about amateurish "Bigfoot science" divorced from disciplined evidence standards.

If legitimate proof ever surfaces, the damage inflicted by premature announcements might well delay mainstream acceptance substantially. For now the Sasquatch Genome Project controversy remains a cautionary tale in a genre already struggling against stigma. But for some loyal followers, Ketchum's willingness to risk reputation still makes her a pioneer seeking truths the establishment denies. Unless others can replicate her DNA findings, the claims seem destined to linger on the fringes as a quixotic quest blind to its own hubris.

The Olympic Project: Seeking Proof in Washington's Remote Peninsula

The Pacific Northwest's remote Olympic Peninsula has accumulated Bigfoot accounts for over a century, from indigenous tales through pioneer journals to a consistent chronicle among remote logging camps and national park rangers of encounters with giant "wild men" lurking deep in the primeval rainforests blanketing the interior.

Seeking to finally document these decades of sightings, a research group called The Olympic Project coalesced in 2009 around a unifying mission - to leverage latest technologies and scientific methodology in a multiyear field study seeking definitive proof of the elusive cryptid.

In this chapter we explore TOP's unique origins, field work approach, use of technology, perspective on why conclusive evidence remains elusive, and their plans to marshal proof if obtained to compel government action securing Bigfoot scientific protection.

History and Approach

TOP emerged organically from online Bigfoot forums by Washington state residents familiar with the long history of sightings on the Olympic Peninsula. Rather than casual hobbyists, founding members brought expertise in engineering, biochemistry, anthropology and veterinary sciences to bear on designing rigorous field study protocols borrowing from wildlife population research.

They focused efforts in the remote southeastern quadrant of the vast peninsula where the 1994 Bigfoot sighting by Forest Service employee Bill Hall gained fame, as well as the Lake Cushman area. Their approach emphasized establishing control survey grids to facilitate repeatable transects year-over-year using latest cameras and DNA sampling techniques.

While lacking direct university affiliations, TOP collaborates respected primatologists, biologists and wildlife officials to bring heightened scientific rigor to their initiatives spanning over a decade now while keeping an open mind to Native American perspectives on the spiritual "wild people" still claimed to inhabit the ancient forests.

Field Work and Technology Use

TOP conducts multiple week-long expeditions into remote Olympic park lands each year, accessing areas by foot. Ground teams perform grid sweeps looking for structures, tracks or nests. Perimeter camera traps use AI sensing to maximize image captures. Drones and FLIR sensors scan ridge lines and valleys for heat and motion anomalies. Passive audio devices record sounds for analysis by acoustic experts. Hair traps and organic material get stored for university DNA testing seeking sequences indicating rare primates.

While TOP has yet to secure that pivotal video or DNA sample proving Bigfoot's existence, the group remains confident their methodical approach leveraging maturing technologies improves odds yearly. They compile annual technical reports documenting all evidence pieces - however inconclusive individually - to identify patterns consistent with a living species leaving its trace.

Why No Definitive Proof Yet?

Like all long-term Bigfoot projects, TOP fields the inevitable question of why irrefutable documentation still eludes them after over a decade scouring the remote rainforests of the Olympic range. They reflect similar theories as other groups: small scattered bands inhabiting thick canopy forest across rough terrain spanning thousands of square miles thwarts easy discovery. The peninsula likely hosts no more than a few dozen individuals at most.

But TOP remains dedicated to the premise that diligent science must prevail eventually. As AI-enabled cameras, drones and DNA sequencing continue rapidly advancing, the probability of capturing multiple clear images or genetic confirmation of anomaly primates rises accordingly. When the evidence reaches critical mass, they feel mainstream rejection will crumble in the data deluge soon to come.

Preparing for Protection

Once definitive proof surfaces, TOP plans to immediately engage Washington state and federal officials as well as university primatologists to ensure Bigfoot gets designated an endangered species. This would activate legal frameworks preventing harm or capture of the creatures, while launching population census efforts to map their range for ongoing monitoring and conservation management.

Of course much remains unpredictable how such famously reclusive giants would react to such schemes enacted in their name. But TOP aims first to prove their reality through science rather than legend. Where the story goes next remains unwritten till the elusive beast itself authors the ending.

Why No Body?

The Everlasting Mystery of Missing Sasquatch Remains

Of all the lingering questions complicating acceptance of Sasquatch's existence, one towers above the rest: where are the bodies? Without tangible physical remains – whether skeletal fossils, preserved tissue, or even a corpse – mainstream science refuses to acknowledge the reality of a giant undiscovered ape roaming North America alongside humans for centuries.

Believers argue that sustained eyewitness accounts across decades, corroborating video footage, and other trace evidence should suffice to prove these creatures exist in some capacity. But the lack of irrefutable physical proof continues allowing skeptics to relegate Bigfoot to fantasy or folklore. No bodies means no definitive zoological classification or scientific acceptance.

In this chapter, we dive deep on why no Sasquatch bodies have emerged. We explore the key challenges around finding and retrieving physical remains, profile how their behavior as an intelligent species hampers discovery, and assess conspiracy theories around alleged government suppression of tangible evidence.

By examining the mystery of the missing bodies from various angles, can we get closer to understanding why science has yet to produce that one breakthrough piece of tangible proof to crack the Bigfoot code once and for all?

The Challenges Finding and Retrieving Remains

Any quest to produce a Sasquatch type specimen or skeletal set capable of convincing science must first acknowledge the immense obstacles facing such physical evidence coming to light:

- Harsh Climate – The Pacific Northwest climate, where most Bigfoot activity occurs, receives over 100 inches of rainfall annually. Between precipitation and flooding, remains likely decompose rapidly.
- Dense Vegetation – Heavily forested areas also accelerate decomposition and allow remains to be consumed quickly by scavengers.
- Remoteness – With a small overall population spread thinly across vast wilderness, the odds of finding a body before deterioration remains astronomical.
- No Migration Paths – Unlike species like elephants that use known seasonal migration routes where remains occasionally accumulate, Bigfoot show no such patterns that allow for discoveries.
- Restricted Access – Rugged, roadless terrain makes mounting search efforts logistically unfeasible.
- Taboo Topic – The stigma surrounding Bigfoot also discourages academics from touching the topic out of fear of ridicule, leaving few qualified experts searching.

When the climate, geography, population density, and cultural attitudes align against proof surfacing, it's easier to understand why physical evidence has yet to emerge. But other aspects of Sasquatch behavior and biology likely also contribute.

How Bigfoot Behavior Hampers Finds

If Bigfoot evolved intelligence akin to the great apes, certain behaviors passed down may offer clues that also inhibit their remains from being found:

- Wariness of Humans – If Sasquatch perceive humans as threats, they likely have developed skills to evade detection that also serve to conceal themselves in death.
- Removal of Dead – Many primates have cultural tendencies to bury or hide dead members of their troop which could explain the lack of Bigfoot carcasses.
- Nocturnal Habits – As primarily nocturnal creatures in the reports, their darkness-dwelling ways also avoid detection and remain hidden in death.

- Nomadic Existence – Living nomadically in small bands allows dying members to isolate themselves in remote areas, avoiding skeletal discovery.
- Wild Diet – Foraging on wild vegetation means no livestock tagging as in other grazers, further obscuring migration habits and range.
- These behaviors mesh with survival for a rare species, but also perfectly align to prevent their remains from being uncovered.
- Bigfoot may also hold certain biological advantages to avoid leaving behind skeletal evidence:
- Dense Bones – Some analyses suggest a very large Bigfoot skeleton could actually fossilize rapidly, leading to mineralization of bones.
- Toothlessness – Theoretically, a ridgeless jaw structure would leave no teeth fossils to be discovered.
- Burial Instincts – Primates often bury their dead deliberately, suggesting most Bigfoot skeletons would lay hidden purposefully.

When scientific understanding lags so far behind their advanced abilities, the deck remains stacked against finding an actual body. But could more sinister forces also be at play to hide the physical reality of Bigfoot?

Government Conspiracy Theories

A popular sentiment in some cryptozoology circles is that the government – whether at federal or state levels – actively suppresses or hides Bigfoot evidence from public view in order to allow the species to remain undisturbed. They believe the truth is being covered up by land management agencies.

- Specific theories vary but share core premises around the discovery of bodies or captives:
- Federal Government Collusion – After reports of Bigfoot bodies recovered, an order from top levels demands evidence seized and hidden to avoid chaos.

- State Government Hiding – Local authorities in areas with frequent sightings secretly collect and destroy remains on orders from higher up.
- National Security Threat – The military views validation of Bigfoot as a threat to public safety near bases and wants proof buried.
- Environmental Cover-Up – Government agencies charged with land stewardship realize Bigfoot populations are extremely fragile and evidence must be suppressed to ensure protective isolation.

While dramatic theories can be alluring, most lack hard evidence beyond circumstantial accounts. And the vastness of potential habitat plus scientific obstacles seem more realistic explanations for the lack of bodies rather than broad collusion. But until a specimen emerges, doubt will linger for some.

Bridging the Gap

In the end, the absence of definitive Bigfoot remains comes down to an equation based on known species behaviors and predicted biology – but influenced heavily by logistical barriers to discovery sites. Their evolutionary path as intelligent, ultra-elusive hominids adept at concealment simply leads inevitably to a lack of verifiable physical evidence.

Powerful instincts drive Bigfoot to isolate themselves in death and perhaps even purposefully hide their remains from human discovery. And the climate, geography and tiny scattered populations across an unforgiving landscape do the rest to prevent science from finally glimpsing total proof.

But in a realm still governed more by legend than fact, the door remains open for new evidence. As researchers implement more sophisticated technologies like thermal drones, remote trail cameras sensing motion and heat, and even Bigfoot call blasting to isolate acoustical signatures, the odds may slowly shift. The absence of bodies may yet transform from endlessly elusive to finally found. For those who believe the Sasquatch walks among us, the search continues for the missing piece stumping mainstream science.

Conclusion

Connecting the Strands of a Compelling Mystery

Across the preceding pages, we have traced the long, winding saga of the legendary creature known as Bigfoot or Sasquatch - from Native American lore and early pioneer accounts to famous film footage and disputed discoveries that tease but never quite satisfy demands for conclusive scientific proof.

Like a fog enshrouded in the ancient forest, the giant hominid slips between accepted reality and dismissed fantasy, neither fully materializing nor completely vanishing. As this book went to print, global sightings surpassed over 10,000 accumulated reports with hundreds more emerging annually. And yet among all the alleged signs and traces documented, the central figure remains ephemeral - seeming almost to taunt efforts that seek to definitively reveal its true nature once and for all.

But rather than proof, perhaps the enduring mystery compels us most to reflect on our relationship with this obscure beast - why it continues to entrance imaginations and defiantly resists categories. What explains the relentless drive by generations to resolve an uncertainty that thrives on eluding certainty?

In this conclusion, we step back to connect the strands that collectively argue for existence despite the absence of a body. We revisit the key themes that tantalize if not conclusively confirm; the evidence that convinces some but not all. And in appraising the case built link by link, the silhouette of a giant takes form if we choose to see its shape looming behind the veil between legend and reality. There may be more unknown than we can currently grasp.

If Bigfoot were simply a cultural myth spawned randomly over centuries, would not stories vary wildly with radical differences in descriptions and behaviors reported? Instead the relative consistency across accounts proves striking - especially between early indigenous oral traditions passed down through generations and modern eyewitness testimonies facilitated by instant communications.

Both historical and recent narratives describe a giant hairy hominid walking upright on two legs, towering from eight to even twelve feet tall. It smells pungently, emits piercing cries, shies violently from humans, and disappears swiftly into deep forests. The behavior aligns perfectly with an intelligent but less technologically advanced species threatened by mankind and seeking to avoid contact at all costs. Too many common themes emerge not to warrant a deeper look.

The Sheer Volume of Sightings

But could eyewitness testimony alone ever substantiate a new species given human fallibility? Skeptics argue the fallible human mind superimposes patterns upon randomness. Yet the sheer number of reports countermands casual dismissal.

Believers ask what constitutes sufficient quantity to overcome doubt. 10 sightings? 100? 1000? No firm barometer exists to shift folklore into zoology. But how many hoaxes, lies and mistakes stay hidden for long? The fame and fortune tempting publicity never emerged despite 10,000+ accounts on record. And the consistent eyewitness types reporting - park rangers, police, biologists, experienced hunters and trackers familiar with wildlife - beg harder questions around origins.

The Credibility of Certain Evidence Cases

If even ninety-nine of a hundred trackways discovered prove admittedly questionable, could not the one-percent displaying scientifically perplexing traits still point to something unproven watching from the forests? Examples like the Cripplefoot prints and the disputed Skookum Cast at least deserve deeper consideration rather than knee-jerk rejection. And the dermal ridges visible on certain casts remain consistent with primate friction skin telling of their passing.

No single video or photo may convince in isolation. But the accumulated hours of alleged footage containing common movement patterns and anatomical features again argue an elusive giant hominid manifests more substantially than myth. And the consistent remote wilderness locations of sightings, nests, and tracks lend further credibility that these secluded habitats conceal a shy beast fading towards extinction before fully substantiated.

The Vastness of Potential Habitat

Critics counter that despite tens of thousands of trail cameras monitoring North American forests in recent years, no definitive Bigfoot evidence emerged to silence skeptics. They argue that in today's interconnected world, an unrecognized giant mammal proves preposterous regardless of wilderness acreage remaining.

Yet believers point to the Pacific Northwest's vast tracts of undeveloped land still cloaked in old growth rainforest or soaring peaks that deter surveillance by man or machines. The remoteness spans far wider than the limited zones subject to intense monitoring. Could small tribes still roam free there as shadows of a lost age?

And great apes inhabit only tropical niches right? But relict populations cut off from ancestral ranges adapt new behaviors and habitats. If Bigfoot descended from Gigantopithecus, might it have evolved thick fur coats to brave frozen winters across eons? Survival drives life to overcome assumed constraints. Too much unknown landscape remains to declare the species impossible with certainty.

Bigfoot at the Crossroads

In the end, the case for Bigfoot's reality seems poised at a crossroads in the second decade of the 21st century - pushed to the cusp of validation by cultural momentum yet still denied the definitive proof science requires. As exponential advances in genetics, surveillance and population modeling flood cryptozoology, the giant hominid's days of roaming undetected draw inevitably to a close.

Yet in this transitional moment, the romantic in us pauses to wonder: will conclusively documenting the species finally end the eons of mystery around a creature that refuses to materialize fully before our lenses? Will its power as a cultural emblem diminish once the chase concludes and it joins other endangered species struggling to avoid extinction?

Perhaps Bigfoot's enduring hold on our collective imagination arises not from elusiveness alone but also its symbolism of the unknown watching from the borderlands. Of nature still concealing profound secrets if we dare tread quietly enough into the ancient forest gloom. There may remain realities not yet ripe for our comprehension. Unknowns that shape shift when dragged fully into the light.

For those seeking hard evidence, the quest continues to reveal the tangibility behind this great legend. But for others more attuned to life's intangible mysteries, the giant that haunts our collective unconscious may always lurk more powerfully in imagination's penumbra - neither proven nor disproven but rather felt palpably in the stillness of a primeval wood. Always just glimpsed, never grasped. In that sense, perhaps we should tread cautiously lest we trap an embodiment of the unknown best left to wander wild in our dreams.

For more books by Jamie visit www.areghostsreal.info

Made in the USA
Middletown, DE
12 March 2024